BEAUTY FOR ASHES

NAILAH AGYEMANN

Beauty for Ashes
Copyright © 2024 by Nailah Agyemann

All rights reserved. Printed in the United States of America. No part of this book may be used or reproduced in any manner whatsoever without written permission except in the case of brief quotations embodied in critical articles and reviews. Permission granted on request.

Qui 2 Life Publishing
34 Shining Willow Way
LaPlata, MD 20646
www.qui2life.com
1 (301) 710-5219

Print ISBN: 979-8-9869513-4-8

eBook ISBN: 979-8-9869513-5-5

Library of Congress Cataloging-in-Publication

Author Name: Nailah Agyemann

Title: Beauty for Ashes

Edited by: Tania Easterling and T. Lynn Tate

Cover Design by: Olayemi Bolaji

Qui 2 Life Publishing is not responsible for any content or determination of work. All information is solely considered as the point of view of the author.

Scriptures taken from Holy Bible, King James, Message, and NIV versions at Biblegateway.com, Public Domain.

This book is dedicated to all of those lost souls who are adrift in the sea of life. I pray you can find an anchor in Matthew 7:7 ASK it shall be given to you. SEEK and you shall find. KNOCK and the door shall be open. Lastly, I dedicate this book to little Carla and all the children that have and/or are living through sexual, emotional, verbal, and physical abuse.
WE ARE SURVIVORS!!!

Acknowledgments

Giving honor to my Lord and Savior Jesus Christ, it is out of obedience to the Holy Spirit that this book was written. I give my all to you, Lord.

Next, I thank my mother, Selma Kennedy. Though we have not always seen eye to eye, you have always been there for me when I needed you. Your love for me has been steadfast and unmovable. I love you mama.

To my sister and first best friend, Karen, as children you were my first confidante. We shared secrets that only sisters can understand. As adults, you are a guiding light on my spiritual journey.

Akosua and Tariq, you are my greatest achievements. Through all the strife we have been through I would not change it for anything. It is what has made us stronger. I love being your mommy.

To Artise, my first love. May love, peace and joy be with you eternally. You are truly missed. Rest easy my friend.

To all my family and friends too numerous to name, I value and love you beyond measure.

Lastly, to my publisher, T Lynn Tate, through this entire process of penning the book, you consoled me when I became emotional, encouraged me when it became too hard, and celebrated with me when the book was completed. Thank you for being my friend and publisher.

To the staff at Qui 2 Life Publishing, I humbly say thank you for all you do.

I AM A WOMAN OF GOD

The road to this place in my life has been filled with mistakes, misfortunes, missteps, failures, successes, lessons and blessings. Through it all, God kept me. The story you're about to read is not just a story, it's my journey to becoming the woman that God had predestined and purposed me to be. Today, I submit myself as a living testament to God's goodness, love, protection, and provision. He truly took my ashes and exchanged them for beauty in Him.

CHAPTER ONE

Thursday, August 29, 1957, Congress passed the first Civil Rights Act into law in 82 years. This law authorized the attorney general to file lawsuits on behalf of African Americans denied the right to vote. As monumental as that event was in the nation's capital, something far more spectacular happened in another part of the city. "Nete" and "Nut" welcomed the first of their two daughters, me, Carla Denise Kennedy.

My family lived on Grant Street in the Parkside Garden projects of Northeast, DC for six wonderful years. We filled life with as much fun as a kid could have. I have countless memories of playing outdoors for what seemed like forever, especially in the summer. The kids in the neighborhood played tag, red light, hide and seek, jump rope, and many other childhood games.

The adage, "It takes a village to raise a child," was true in my neighborhood. Our entire neighborhood looked out for all the kids, so much so that word of my misbehaving always reached home before I did. Our neighbors permitted us into their homes for a drink of water or to take a break from playing. As kids, we knew if we went home, we couldn't come back out until much later, and we were having way too much fun to stop playing.

In our neighborhood, they hung hand-washed clothes outside on clotheslines to dry. I can still smell the freshness of the clothes as they came off the line. One day, I was swinging on the clothesline pole, having a good ole time, until I lost my grip. Bam! I went down and hit the concrete so hard that my front tooth cut into my bottom lip. I was terrified by the sight of all the blood that poured from my mouth. A neighbor saw what happened, picked me up, and brought me home to my father.

As I lay on the couch crying for my mommy, the only words of comfort my father shared were don't go to sleep or else you'll die. What a horrible thing to tell a distraught child. Of course, later, I found out he was concerned I may have had a concussion and told me I would die to keep me awake. But in that moment, my young mind needed comfort, not more fear. Eventually, they took me to the hospital, and I received several stitches in my lip. I bear the scar from that accident to this day.

My community had block parties and neighborhood-wide cookouts in the summer. The food, fun, and games were plentiful. I heard the sound of Motown Records everywhere as the adults grooved to the music of the Temptations, the Supremes, and the Four Tops, just to name a few. We didn't have a swimming pool, so they opened the fire hydrants on hot and humid days for the kids to play in the water.

Our neighbor across the street, Mr. White, cooked hotdogs, hamburgers, and chicken on the grill. The smell of the food traveled throughout the "hood." Other neighbors would chip in and bring various side dishes to complete the meal. Since I didn't like onions, my mother always made a small batch of potato salad just for me. Mr. White's grill became like a campfire in the evenings for the kids to roast marshmallows on sticks.

Life was good until it wasn't. When I was about four years old, I accidentally set myself on fire. My mother was in the kitchen fixing a snack for me and my sister, Karen. It was fruit cake and milk. Sitting in the living room, I found a book of matches on the sofa under the newspaper. The babysitter had left them there, and I later blamed them for my burns.

With the curiosity of a child, I swiped the match against the striking surface, and to my surprise, the match lit up. I didn't know what to do with it, so I laid it on my dress, which had a highly flammable crinoline slip underneath. Immediately, my dress went up in flames with me in it.

Karen, a toddler, said, "Carla on fire," but my mother didn't hear her.

So, Karen said again, "Momma, Carla on fire."

My mother looked from the kitchen and saw a ball of flames, me screaming on the sofa. She rushed from the kitchen to help me.

She screamed, "Nut, Carla is on fire!"

My father was upstairs asleep, and I was unsure how long it took him to get downstairs. I also don't know how my mother had the presence of mind to know exactly what to do to extinguish the flames. I believe it was God and the motherly instincts he gives mothers to rescue their babies when in trouble.

My mother extinguished the fire and me, but not before both of us sustained severe burns. I had second-degree burns on my right forearm, right thigh, and stomach. Above my right elbow, I suffered a third-degree burn, which serves today as one of several childhood battle scars. My mother also received second-degree burns on her arm and hand.

My mother and I rode to the hospital together in the ambulance. I just knew they would put a cast on my arm. In my childhood resilience, I was ecstatic at the thought of a cast. My family and I could write and draw pictures on it; at least, that's what I thought. My grandparents were already at the hospital when we arrived. Despite the worry that covered their faces, I was so glad to see Granny and Day.

To my disappointment, I did not get a cast because they don't use plaster on burns. Instead, I received bandages that allowed airflow to help heal the wounds. I had to have my bandages changed every so often to prevent infection. Naturally, the bandages weren't as fun as the cast would have been.

To this day, I still have a taste aversion toward fruit cake and milk because of my terrible experience. Although I have healed physically, the mental trauma I sustained left a foul taste in my mouth for what was my favorite snack. Little did I know more mental and emotional trauma was headed my way.

My mom worked the night shift at a nursing home, which left my father to care for my sister and I. It was during this time my father began sexually abusing me. I am not sure how old I was when the abuse started, but I believe I was about 3-4 years old. Although many of the surrounding memories are vague, some are still quite vivid.

I remember lying on my mother's bed numb as my father laid on top of me. The smell of alcohol was strong on his breath as he gyrated in me. Past him, I could see the sun as it shined through the window and heard the kids outside playing as the music blared from the small box radio on my parent's dresser. This is the memory that stays with me the most. It, along with many other suppressed memories, led to many years of unresolved trauma.

I began my primary education at Nevel Thomas Elementary School. My first teacher was Ms. Hancock. For the longest time, I thought her name was Ms. Handcuff. She made a great impression on my life with the way she encouraged and nurtured my love of reading. My mother taught me to read at an early age. By the time I started kindergarten, I read on a first-grade level. I still have a love for reading to this day.

As I was headed to the first grade, my family moved from Grant Street. But we didn't all move together. I'm not sure what happened between my parents, but they decided to go their separate ways. There was never a real discussion about it. Maybe they grew apart as some high school sweethearts do. Nevertheless, my mom, my sister, and I were on our own.

We moved a few times after we left Grant Street. We settled into an apartment on Horner Place in Southeast DC when I was in second grade. My mother befriended a neighbor named Miss Sharon, who had several children, some of whom would babysit me and my sister. Now, Miss Sharon was separated from her husband, Greg, but he controlled her and their kids as if he lived there.

Occasionally, we would sleep over at their house

when our mothers went out for girls' night. It was during this time Miss Sharon's son, Lance, began to sexually abuse me. He would take me to the basement, lay me on the bed, and have his way with me.

Somehow, my young mind tried to equate what happened to me as a relationship. After one of the basement sessions, I told Lance he was my boyfriend. As I look back, what did I know about a boyfriend? I guess saying he was my boyfriend made me feel better and "justified" about what was happening to me. The simple truth was the apple hadn't fallen far from the tree, and I just happened to be the naïve recipient.

One night, my mother had a little get-together at our house and invited Miss Sharon. Since it was a grownups' party, my sister and I stayed at Miss Sharon's house. Greg came over to see Miss Sharon while we watched TV and played games in the house. He asked where she was, and one of the children reluctantly told him.

As the night progressed, we went to bed, but Greg stayed and waited for Miss Sharon to return home. Greg was a barber by profession and owned a neighborhood shop, so he always kept a straight-edge razor with him. He sat in the dark living room and festered in his anger. When Miss Sharon walked in the door, Greg pounced on her, and she never saw it coming.

Greg violently beat and cut his wife while he yelled, cussed, and accused her of infidelity and not doing what he told her to do. In other words, she hadn't obeyed him. Miss Sharon's gut-wrenching screams were heard all throughout the house. She yelled for him to stop and begged her kids or anyone to help her. We cried with her and wanted to help, but we were too terrified to move.

The beating finally stopped, and Greg left the house. The kids rushed to help Miss Sharon, and I called my mom for help. Her cuts were so deep one could see the dermis layer of her skin. She was rushed to the hospital and received stitches for the multiple cuts Greg inflicted on her.

In those days, women, particularly black women, had little to no rights when it came to abusive husbands or boyfriends. Greg didn't live in the home with Miss Sharon. He lived with another woman and their kids. Greg ruled with an unforgiving iron fist. Since he financially provided for Miss Sharon and the kids with food and clothes, he felt he had every right to control their household and terrorize the family.

That incident left an indelible impression on me. To this day, I do not enter my home or any place if the lights are off. My living room light stays on 24 hours a day, 365 days a year. At this point in my life, one would think I would be passed this, but uh-no! I have never forgotten Miss Sharon's screams for help and the sight of her cuts.

CHAPTER TWO

Shortly after the incident, my family moved to a new place a few blocks away. Although my mother and Miss Sharon remained friends and her daughters continued to babysit us, my mom no longer permitted us to stay overnight. This was my mother's way of keeping my sister and I from harm. Unfortunately, Miss Sharon's abuse continued, and so did mine. I never told anyone what Lance was doing to me. The sexual abuse became a regular part of my life, and I no longer saw the wrong in it.

I had emotional scars from more than the sexual abuse. Let me preface what I'm about to share. My mother was a single parent and did the best she could to raise two girls. She made sure we had shelter, food, and clothes. She sacrificed herself to ensure all our needs and some of our wants were met. I can't recall a special occasion where we didn't receive anything.

However, although she was a great provider, she was not demonstrative or expressive towards us with her love.

My mom thought it was enough to have our physical needs met, and that was how she expressed her love. As a child, I did not understand having my basic needs met was a form of love. I thought that was the basic responsibility of a mother and what she was supposed to do. I needed and wanted to hear the words I love you as well as feel that I was loved.

We were never told what happened between my parents that caused them to separate, but I felt like my mom took her anger out on us, especially me.

When I didn't understand something in school or got something wrong, she'd say, "You're stupid, just like Nut."

If I didn't clean like she wanted, I was called lazy and trifling. I was called dumb, stupid, lazy, and trifling on what seemed like a regular basis. The first person to ever call me a bitch was my mother, and I have hated that word ever since. If I ever referred to another person by that word, trust and believe they had royally pissed me off. But as a kid, I believed what I heard, especially since it came from my mother. If she said I was all those things, they must've been true, right?

The abuse did not stop at verbal. Back in the day, some parents were physically abusive in the name of discipline. If you didn't get beat with a belt, extension cord, shoe, or whatever else parents could get their hands on, you were not disciplined. There was no timeout to think about what you did or stand in the corner for discipline, and you sho'nuff did not get to choose your punishment. No sir, no way.

I'm sure I am not the only person of my generation to get spanked by having their head placed between their mother's thighs with their naked behind exposed. There was no way you could get out of that position without breaking your neck. So, you had no recourse other than to endure the beating you were about to receive. Just the thought of those butt whippings makes me shudder.

Don't get me wrong, life at home wasn't totally unbearable. Sure, as a child, I sometimes felt I lived in a hell hole. Still, I knew my mother did the best she could with what she had to give mentally, physically, and emotionally. And if the truth be told, I had my fair share of inflicting pain as well.

I was a teenager when, one morning, my mom prepared for work. Her morning routine was to set the ironing board up in her room while she took her bath. This particular morning, I ironed my clothes for the day while she was in the tub. I didn't see a problem as the iron sat idle at the time. Mom took issue with me using the iron and began to cuss and yell at me. Without thinking, I took the hot iron and placed it on her back.

Although the iron was on her back for only a few

seconds, it was long enough to leave a permanent scar. At that moment, I did not feel any remorse. I was fed up with the mental and verbal abuse. However, as the years passed, I felt bad about what I did.

There is a running joke in my family about the "bee stinger." Granny had Day create the bee stinger by cutting a leather belt into four thin slices. Instead of you being hit once, you were hit four times. There was nothing worse than Granny telling me to get the bee stinger.

I remember saying, "No granny, not the bee stinger."

Granny was generally very patient with me and all her grandkids, but when the bee stinger came out, I knew her patience was at an end.

I felt like my whole world was crushed each time I was disciplined. I felt unloved and angry, especially when my mother disciplined me. How could she, the person who was supposed to love me, inflict such pain? I suppressed the anger towards my mother deep inside to the point that, at times, I didn't like her. I loved her with all my heart, but I did not like her.

I knew my feelings toward my mom were probably wrong because she was my mother, and I was supposed to love and like her. But as a child, I could not reconcile those conflicted feelings. Unfortunately, that added yet another layer to the unresolved trauma that continuously built within me.

As if my young mind didn't have enough to deal

with, the murder of Dr. Martin Luther King Jr came and took the black communities by storm. I was ten years old when he died, and I vividly remember watching the news of his death on television and seeing the replay of his last speech. The National Guard was stationed at Ballou High School on the hill to give them a vantage point over the neighborhood and surrounding area.

I remember seeing the looting and riots in the neighborhood streets and gleefully asking why we weren't outside.

My mother quickly said, "It's too dangerous. Besides, the city is under a curfew."

I asked, "What is a curfew?"

My mother replied, "It means the city is on lockdown, and we can't be outside after dark."

I had so many questions. Like, why would someone want to kill Dr. King? I was too young to fully understand the Civil Rights movement, but I knew that Dr. King worked to stop the mistreatment of Negroes or "colored" folks as we were known then. It boggled my mind because he died so violently, even though he preached and practiced nonviolent resistance. To this day, I believe my latent militancy was born during that turbulent time, albeit subconsciously.

Not long after Dr. King died, my Aunt Frances and her three sons, Jeffrey, Gerald, and John, affectionately known as "Mickey," moved into our building. My mother had three siblings: Uncle Chuck, Aunt Frances, and Aunt Regina. Since Aunt Frances did not have girls and my mother did not have boys, we were raised more as siblings than cousins.

We lived on the first floor, and Aunt Frances lived on the third floor. It was great to have "brothers" who lived so close. Jeffrey was the oldest and became our new babysitter. I no longer had to endure the sexual abuse from Lance because the predator was removed from my life when my cousin became my sitter.

CHAPTER THREE

The summer of '69 was one of many changes. It was the year after the Olympics when Tommie Smith and John Carlos raised their black-gloved fists in solidarity with the Black Panthers while the entire world watched. It ushered in the transitional period from Negro to Black Pride for people of color, and James Brown told us in his song to "Say it loud, I'm Black and I'm Proud." More importantly, I graduated from elementary school and looked forward to junior high school with my friends. Unbeknownst to me, my mother had other plans.

My family followed Aunt Frances, and we moved to a different part of Southeast, Randle Highland, into a brand new and modern apartment building. The building was so new that we were the first family to reside in our unit. These apartments had all the amenities one could want—individually controlled heat and air, wall-to-wall carpet, garbage disposal, patio, and, last but not least, an onsite laundry room. We no longer needed to haul dirty clothes to the laundromat to wash, dry, and fold. For two strong single black women providing for their families, Frances and Nete won gold medals with these apartments, and it wasn't even an Olympic year.

The thought of starting a new school without any friends terrified me to no end. Although my cousin Gerald and I attended the same school, he was too cool to be seen with his nerdy cousin. In the seventh grade, I wore glasses, had knobby knees, and still wore plaits in my hair. I'm talking the standard one plait on top, two parted down the middle in the back, and each braided with a barrette on the end to keep it from unraveling. As if that wasn't enough, I was flat-chested, which added to my childlike appearance. I was an awkward, self-conscious, shy black girl and felt like an ugly duckling.

My junior high school was two miles round trip from home, and I walked to school daily. It amazes me how, back then, I walked those two miles with no problem, but today, I struggle to walk two blocks. Whew chile, if only I had my youthfulness again. Anyway, when school started that September, Gerald walked with me because the distance was too far for me to walk alone. That, of course, cramped his style. As I stated previously, he did not want to be seen with his nerdy cousin. After all, someone might think I was his girlfriend, and we couldn't have that rumor ruin his image.

Once Gerald and I got to school, I was on my own, which was a big feat for me. Eventually, I made friends once I discovered I was not the only person who felt out of place. My English teacher assigned me to work on a group project. This was where I found my first school friend. Her name was Constance.

The group project involved a lot of reading, which we both loved to do. But we really bonded when she found out the boy she had a crush on lived in my neighborhood, and he and I were friends. Back then, if you had a big afro and were bowlegged, you were considered very attractive. Well, Phillip, the object of Constance's desire, was all that. The icing on the cake for her was that he was light-skinned (the issue of colorism within the black race is a whole other subject). I told Phillip that my friend liked him.

Phillip's response really surprised me. He told me he was not interested in Connie because he liked me. You can only imagine how I felt. Here was the boy I knew from the neighborhood, and I had no idea he liked me. I thought we were just neighborhood friends.

When I told Connie that Phillip did not like her but me, she said, "I stole her boyfriend."

I told her he was not her boyfriend and it was not my fault he liked me and not her. Connie's and my friendship was not the same after Phillip and I started going together.

Although Phillip and I knew each other from the neighborhood, we did not really know each other well. When we talked on the phone, we realized we had two things in common. Both of us were in the seventh grade and still sucked our thumbs. Yes, I was a thumb sucker in junior high school. The habit soothed and comforted me. I felt relieved to find out my new boyfriend was a thumb sucker as well.

When some of the "cool" and popular girls in school found out Phillip was my boyfriend, they looked at me with such disdain. Secretly, I laughed inside because the ugly, dark-skinned, nerdy girl had one of the cutest sought-after boys in school as her boyfriend. I did not choose him. He chose me. I was not allowed to have boyfriends until I was sixteen. So, at thirteen, I kept the true nature of my friendship a secret from my mother. I couldn't tell any adult, not even my beloved grandmother, whom I trusted with all my heart.

My grandparents were an integral part of my upbringing. Every year, for my birthday, Granny baked my favorite yellow cake with chocolate icing from scratch. She never used box mix or canned icing.

The family celebrated every holiday at my grandparent's home. On Thanksgiving, the aroma of the turkey in the oven met you at the door. Freshly cooked greens were on the stove, baked and buttered rolls cooled on the table, and delectable goodies waited to be devoured.

For New Year's Eve, we played Pokeno and Bingo, drank eggnog, and stayed up to watch Lawrence Welk as we brought the New Year in. This was the grandkids' tradition with our grandparents while our parents had a night out to celebrate. I have so many fond memories of me, my sister, and my cousins with them.

On December 10, 1969, my beloved grandfather, Day, died. I still remember that day as if it were yesterday. It was gloomy and cold both in weather and emotion. We had finished our school day, and my cousin Jeffrey told Karen and I to come to their apartment, which wasn't an unusual request.

Once we got there, we all sat around the dining table, and he told us Day had died. Immediately, I began to cry. This was the first time anyone close to me had passed away. We knew Day was sick because we visited him in the veteran's hospital, but as children, we thought he would come home after the doctors made him better.

My mom and her siblings helped my grandmother make the funeral arrangements. They wanted the funeral to take place before the week of Christmas to give us kids a sense of normalcy. Despite their best effort to make everything as normal as possible, it just was not the same. My grandfather Day was not there to celebrate with us.

We continued our tradition of spending New Year's Eve with Granny, so she would not bring in the New Year alone. As I got older, I came to think the grayness of that day was symbolic of the news that awaited me.

My grandparents had a deep and abiding love. Their bond was unbreakable. Granny had a difficult time adjusting to life without Day. Jeffrey, who was in high school, moved in with her to ease the difficulty of living alone. The younger grandkids were envious of him because he got to see Granny every day and eat her delicious cooking regularly. She seemed better adjusted with Jeff living with her.

In the fall of '71, Granny visited Denver on a church excursion. On the return trip home, she suffered a stroke. It left her paralyzed on her right side and with slurred speech. For six months, she lived in a nursing home in Wheaton, MD.

One day, Karen, Aunt Regina, and I went to visit Granny in the home. Aunt Regina wheeled Granny to the patio outside.

Granny said, "I have to go to the bathroom."

Aunt Regina saw a nurse down the hall attending to another patient.

She went to the nurse and said, "Mrs. Davis needs to go to the bathroom."

Without turning to see who was talking to her, the nurse shot back, "Well, Mrs. Davis will have to wait."

Aunt Regina retorted, "Pee on yourself, Mama. They will have to clean you up."

As soon as the nurse realized the patient's family member was talking to her and not one of her co-workers, she quickly changed her tone and tune. She immediately apologized for her comment and found someone to assist my grandmother.

It was too late. The damage had been done, and Aunt Regina reported what happened to my mother and Aunt Frances. They collectively decided to take Granny out of the nursing home and brought her back to our apartment. This meant Karen and I had to share our room with Granny. We each had our own bed to sleep in before, but that changed when Granny moved in. As long as Granny was out of that hell hole of a nursing home, I don't think either of us cared that we shared one twin bed.

Granny lived with us for seven months. A home health aide, Miss Anderson, was hired to care for her during the day. While she lived with us, one of her happiest moments was seeing Jeff in his cap and gown after his high school graduation. She lit up at the sight of her first grandchild in his graduation attire. Her smile could be seen from miles and miles away.

Granny passed away six months later. I was home from school with the flu while Miss Anderson prepared Granny for a doctor's appointment. Aunt

Regina came over to assist Miss Anderson with Granny's care. Although the heat was on, Granny was shivering and said she was cold, but she also felt hot to the touch.

Aunt Regina took Granny's temperature with one of those old glass mercury thermometers. Granny shivered so much the thermometer broke in her mouth, but not before it registered that she in fact had a fever. Concerned that she might have caught the flu from me, Aunt Regina called for an ambulance to take her to the emergency room. Shortly after arriving, the paramedics pronounced Granny dead. She passed in Regina's arms.

As soon as I heard she died, I ran into my mother's room, fell on her bed, and cried. I was so angry with God for taking my grandmother. I was fifteen, and I had lost the person whom I loved more than life. Granny died on December 15, 1972, three years and five days after her beloved husband, Day. The official cause of death was a hardening of the arteries. However, I do not quite believe that was the cause in its entirety.

In the days leading up to the anniversary of my grandfather Day's passing, Granny's mood changed. She seemed quiet and sullen. I have long believed she was still heartbroken over losing the love of her life and did not want to be without him any longer. The day she died was the date we buried her husband and my grandfather three years prior. To me, that was significant.

I believe Granny willed herself to live past his death anniversary in an attempt to spare the family too much pain. Yes, physiologically, she died from hardening of the arteries, but emotionally, she died from the strong desire to be with Day. That was the power of their unbreakable bond. My anger with God over this matter would continue for many years to come.

CHAPTER
FOUR

My cousin Mickey introduced me to Debra. Debbie was one of the cool and popular girls in my neighborhood. I would've given my left arm and right leg to be cool like her.

At our introduction, she said, "I remember you. You were the one I laughed at that day. I saw you walk to school in a plaid coat and white rain hat on your head."

Debbie had a charming, funny, and loveable personality, and it was easy to get to know her. She was an only child and loved spending time with us. We always had so much fun. Debbie, Karen, and I would make up songs and dance routines, then perform them in our living room. Granny lived with us by this time, and we performed our shows for her entertainment. Debbie and I spent the night at each other's houses, where we would have junk food parties, watch TV, and stay up late talking about boys. I mean, what else was there for teenage girls to talk about?

Debbie was such a part of our family. She attended church, sang in the junior choir, and got baptized with us. My mom and Granny even claimed her as their other daughter and granddaughter. Debbie really took to Granny because her grandmother lived in Alabama. We were thick as thieves, for sure.

I remember this one time Debbie and I planned to skip school. We intended to use our lunch money to catch the bus and meet up with some boys. Well, Granny overheard Debbie and I on the phone making our plans.

With her slurred speech, Granny said, "No!"

Her voice shocked me because it was so loud and clear; we did not skip school as planned.

In school, we learned about the dangers of drug use, especially marijuana, also known as weed or herb. They called it the gateway drug. I was twelve when I told my mother that I would never use drugs, drink alcohol, or smoke cigarettes.

My mom said, "You better not," as she blew out cigarette smoke and took a sip from her drink.

Within two years, all that had changed. Debbie always had an adventurous side to her. She began to smoke weed with other kids in the neighborhood. We used to go to the recreation center to hang out after school. It was there they would light up as I stood by and watched. I would ask Debbie questions about how smoking weed made her feel.

She said, "It makes me feel loopy and makes me laugh."

Laugh, they did. It seemed like everything was funny to them when they were smoking, and then they were always looking for something to eat.

At first, I didn't know that being around them meant I could get a contact high. However, once I found out, it didn't stop me from being around them when they smoked. It scared me to actually "hit the joint," but I wanted to participate in the fun. The group persuaded me to take "shotguns," which was when someone took a puff of the joint and then blew it in your face to inhale. In my mind, I was not smoking. I simply breathed in the smoke. Silly me, taking shotguns had the same effect on the mind as actually smoking the joint.

Since I had adverse reactions to alcohol, it wasn't long before I leaped from shotguns to smoking joints. Alcohol had a dangerous effect on me. I would get sick and throw up if I drank too much on an empty stomach. This is the reason I stayed away from alcohol, at least until I learned how to handle drinking much later in life.

I began to skip school in the ninth grade and attend daytime parties. The kids who skipped school would pool their lunch money together to get weed, beer, liquor, and junk food. Then, we'd hang out until it was time to get out of school and go home. I skipped so many days; I had to attend summer school to pass the ninth grade.

Summer school was not the only punishment I received for skipping school so much. My mother decided that it was time for me to change schools. I would no longer attend Anacostia High School, where all my friends went. Instead, she sent me across town to Eastern High School, where I knew no one. Here I was again, going to a new school where I had no friends. It felt like the summer of '69, only worse. My mom's rationale was if my friends weren't around, I would go to school. Little did she know that was far from the truth.

Eastern High School was a premier school in Northeast Washington, DC. The Ramblers, as they were called, were known for their football team and marching band. It was, and still is, a massive building situated on a hill in the Capitol Hill area of DC.

I was terrified walking up to the school in September of '72. Once again, I knew no one, and this was daunting for a shy and self-conscious girl. The school was so huge. I got lost walking from one class to the next and barely made it to class on time.

There was a wall across the street from the school where students would sit and hang out between classes. Although I did not know anyone, I became a regular on the wall. I spent most of my time sitting on the wall during the first few weeks of school, even during some of my classes.

When the season changed from summer to fall, and it began to get cold outside, I would attend the classes I liked. Most of my teachers didn't know who I was. My name was on their class roster, but my face was unfamiliar to them. It made it easy for me to revert to my old ninth-grade habits. So, I left school and went to the daytime parties.

I managed to gain a couple of good friends. One was Sharon, a girl from my neighborhood whose parents had also sent her to Eastern. Then, through her, I reconnected with one of my former sixth-grade classmates, Michelle, who also went to school with us. When I boarded the bus one day, the two of them were sitting on the bus together. I already knew Sharon, so I greeted her and took a seat across from them. Michelle looked at me as if I were familiar to her.

She asked, "Do you have a brother named Gerald?"

I replied, "No, but I have a cousin named Gerald."

Trying to put things together, she asked, "Did you go to Simon Elementary School?"

I said, "Yes."

She said, "I'm Michelle. We were in the same class together in sixth grade."

From that point, our friendship began anew. Michelle was one of the popular and smart girls in our sixth-grade class. She lived in a neighborhood called Trenton Park. I wanted my mom to move us there. It was like anybody who was anybody lived in that development. You were automatically cool and popular when you lived there, or at least that's how it seemed. Back then, Michelle and I were only friends in school. We didn't hang out with each other outside of school.

I attended more of my daily classes after I reconnected with Michelle. However, I still managed to sit on the wall most days. One day after school, Michelle introduced me to her boyfriend, Larry, who, to my surprise, lived on the same street with my great uncle and aunt. As many times as I visited Uncle Pete and Aunt Josephine over the years, I never noticed children outside on their block. I didn't even think kids lived on their street.

Anyway, the two of them decided to play matchmaker. Michelle told me about one of Larry's friends she thought I should meet. Then Larry told his friend that Michelle had a friend he should meet. Eventually, they pulled the right strings and introduced us.

His name was Artise and when we met, I noticed his height, slender build, swag, and self-confidence. We exchanged numbers, and I waited for him to call me. In those days, they considered a girl a "fast tail" if she made the first call. After a few days, he called, and we talked for hours. We talked about a lot of things, but the topic that stuck out the most was our birthdays. His birthdate was four days before mine. At first, I thought he was trying to impress me with a joke.

I said, "Stop playing with me."

He laughed and said, "I'm not. Ok, if you don't believe me, ask Larry."

I did not believe him until Larry confirmed it.

That year, we both turned 16 years old. Artise would walk me to the bus stop a few blocks from the school so we could spend time together. Mind you, there was a bus stop directly across from the school. When I got home from school, I would call to let him know I made it home safely. Then, later that evening, we would talk again for a few more hours.

Karen and I were the first kids in our neighborhood to have a private line in our bedroom. Although she and I shared a phone, ours was separate from my mother's line. Karen hated it when I got on the phone because it meant she couldn't use it for long periods.

I couldn't help myself. I felt a certain way when I talked with Artise. I remember telling Michelle I got warm shivers down my back when he called me baby.

I asked her, "Does that mean I'm in love?"

I had so many questions and what felt like not enough answers. I anxiously awaited Artise's calls, even though I had just left him thirty minutes earlier. This was the first time in my life a male paid that much attention to me without forcing himself on me, and I didn't know what to make of it. Soon, I got the answers to all my questions.

Artise, Michelle, Larry, and I attended Eastern's homecoming football game. In the seventies, the games started immediately after school. Excitement filled the air as we sat, cheering our team on. Suddenly, everyone in the bleachers began to run. I have the old-school mindset that when you see black people running, you run too and ask questions later. I started to run, but Artise grabbed my hand and stopped me. I stopped, turned, and looked at him.

When he touched me, I swear I felt electricity run through my body. When I looked into his eyes, I knew he felt the same way about me. Everything in me told me this was love. We held hands as we ran together.

Later, I asked Artise why he grabbed my hand. He said he didn't want us to get separated, and he did not want me to get hurt. When Artise asked me to be his girlfriend, you would have thought he asked me to marry him. I was so over the moon to be his girlfriend. He was the first boy to see and love me for me.

By the fall of 1974, I was in my third year of the tenth grade. Things were so bad for me at school the assistant principal became my homeroom teacher. This meant I reported to her office every morning and picked up a daily contract. The contract had to be signed by every one of my teachers. It contained questions and comments related to my class participation. It asked questions like was I on time for class, did I do the required homework, and how was my behavior? Then, someone returned the contract to her each day.

The following morning, she and I discussed any negative feedback. Talk about being micromanaged, but I brought this upon myself.

That school year, I decided to get out of the tenth grade. It embarrassed me that my negligent behavior had allowed my sister to catch up with me, and I did not want her to graduate before me. It would have added insult to injury if she left me in high school. Although I hated being micromanaged, it worked for me. I attended every class on time and completed all assignments.

What I didn't know was while I tried to survive micromanagement, my mother advocated for me to attend a different high school. The School Without Walls (SWW) was a non-traditional public high school still in its infancy. Prospective students were interviewed for acceptance. Karen found out about the program in junior high school, interviewed, and got accepted. Upon Karen's acceptance, my mother contacted the SWW principal, Mrs. Caprew, and pleaded my case. I don't know what my mother said, but her words prevailed. The school accepted me without even interviewing me.

CHAPTER
FIVE

I will never forget Mrs. Caprew. Being accepted into SWW made such a big impact on my life. Looking back, I can clearly see how God worked in that situation. SWW was a chance to begin anew, and with my new mindset to get out of the tenth grade, it was the change I needed.

The premise of SWW was they used the entire city as the classroom. The student population consisted of 150 students from diverse backgrounds. It was the first time I attended school with non-black classmates. The school taught traditional classes, such as English, math, and government, for two and a half hours each session. There were also two classes per day instead of seven. This gave the students more time to absorb the materials.

When I say the city was the classroom, literally, that is exactly what it was. For instance, Karen and I got one credit each for Marine Biology and Biochemistry by working on the Lightship Chesapeake. The program took high school students on the Potomac River to explore the river and underwater life. We did experiments with and learned about life aboard a ship.

The ship left port every morning from Ohio Avenue near Hains Point, and they left you behind if you were not in place when the ship departed. Of course, Karen and I learned this the hard way. One time and one time only, Karen and I did not arrive on time. It was a cold winter morning, and we had to walk around Hains Point to find where the ship had docked further downriver for the day's assignment. It took about an hour before we found the ship. They served us hot chocolate to warm our bodies and souls as soon as we boarded. Then, we immediately went to work.

The SWW experience held the best years of my public high school education. The environment at SWW prepared me for college, and the biggest takeaway was the skill of independent study. Each teacher gave us a topic and course outline to follow, but much like writing a semester-long research paper, the work was all on you.

Finally, in the spring of 1977, I graduated from high school. We did not have the traditional class trip or prom. Instead, we attended a small dinner dance. I do not remember where the actual graduation location was, but I recall my mother was equally proud of both her daughters.

In the fall of 1977, I was part of the incoming freshman class of the newly formed University of the District of Columbia (UDC). This was an exciting time for me, as I was on the cusp of adulthood, though I didn't feel like an adult. Artise and I were still together, but he enlisted in the Army when he turned 18. He asked me to marry him, but I was not ready for such a big step. So, we began a long-distance relationship. In the beginning, I remained steadfast to my guy. Over time, it became more and more difficult with him not being around, but I held steadfast for as long as I could.

During the spring semester of my freshman year, I met Henri, and he profoundly impacted me and changed my life. Henri caught my eye one day while I walked to class. The man was so F-I-N-E fine! He had a curly short fro, light amber eyes, and a mischievous smile. He was not slender like Artise, but still, the brother had it going on.

At the suggestion of my English professor, I joined the student government to meet other students. They elected me as freshman class secretary. During one of our student sessions, I discovered Henri was involved in the upper-class student body.

Whether it was en route to class or during student body meetings, I always checked for Henri. One day, I noticed a pair of boots he wore from afar. They were unusual and fashion-trendy—a great conversation starter. But I couldn't bring myself to approach and compliment him. I promised myself if the opportunity presented itself again, I would seize the moment.

Well, on a cold rainy day in early spring, I found Henri leaning against the rail at the bottom of the stairs in the student government building. His back was to me, and as I approached him, I pointed my umbrella at his back.

I said, "This is a stickup. Give me your wallet and keys. I prefer your keys so you can come to my house to get them, and we can get to know each other."

He turned around, flashed that mischievous smile, and replied, "I like how that sounds."

I instantly melted. I don't know what came over me that day or where I even got the opening line and confidence to approach him. However, it worked out for me. We introduced ourselves, and although I never got his keys or wallet, we became good friends.

Henri was sly as a fox. He lived around my old school stomping grounds in Anacostia, Southeast Washington, DC. I still lived at home but would visit Henri since he had his own place. We had some good times hanging out, getting high, and having sex. Henri was a history major with plans to teach history in the DC public schools system. We talked about our African ancestry, history, diaspora, and culture because we both loved history.

Henri's friends were also socially conscious. Many

of them had Afrocentric names and organized local protests. I even protested once with them on Martin Luther King Jr. Avenue. While I do not remember the subject of the protest, I was excited and felt so connected to social activism. I embraced my blackness after that moment.

One of Henri's friends, who was a Rasta, taught me about Rastafarians. Bob Marley and reggae music were all I knew about Rastafarians. However, he taught me that Rastafarianism was more than just a religion. It was a political and cultural lifestyle, and there was much more to it than getting high and dancing to reggae.

It was often said, "You need to connect with a Rasta if you want good weed."

Well, this friend of Henri's had the BEST ganga (weed) around. Smoking a spliff was mind-blowing and took me to another dimension. I felt so free and uninhibited. It was almost spiritual in nature.

I spent so much time with Henri that I no longer attended school or socialized with my friends. My mother worried about my well-being because I stayed away from home so much. Honestly, she thought I had joined a cult the way I acted and spoke of Rastafarianism. She didn't understand the things I talked about because this was in stark contrast to our Christian upbringing.

I embodied the Rastafarianism lifestyle and delved deeper into its history and founding principles. Historically, Rastafarianism began in Jamaica. They believe Haile Selassie I, the Ethiopian Emperor, was the Living God and that black people are the true Israelites and God's chosen people. Dreadlocks are more than a hairstyle. It is the crown and glory where one's spiritual strength lies, and you shouldn't cut them. They also believe white people are evil devil worshippers. Most of all they believed that black people everywhere, in particular the Rastas in Jamaica, should go back to Africa under the rulership of Salassie I.

I spoke with a Bohemian accent and called myself "Irie, the High Priestess of Voodoo," which worried my mother more. Keep in mind I had never been out of the country, nor was I a second-generation American immigrant. Since my friend Debbie knew where Henri lived, my mother asked her to check on me. When Debbie came to visit, my condition appalled her. My appearance was unkept, and I had a lifeless stare. My hair, which was permed, looked like a bird's nest. It was my attempt to grow locs with chemically treated hair, which I now know is impossible.

Debbie knew something wasn't right and insisted I leave with her immediately. I obliged, but after a few hours, I pestered her until she took me back to Henri's place.

Debbie said to my mother, "I'm sorry, but that place just gives me the creeps. I'm worried about her, too, but there's no way I'm going back over there."

My mom and Debbie were right to be concerned.

The more time I spent there, the more I became indoctrinated. I truly believed I was "Irie, the High Priestess of Voodoo." I was a goddess, and Henri was a god. The situation was so bad my mother begged Debbie to return to Henri's place and bring me home. Finally, Debbie gave in and returned, but I refused to leave. So, instead of leaving me there, she stayed with me that night.

The sound of chanting awakened Debbie in the middle of the night. It horrified her to roll over and find someone standing over me, chanting and messing with my foot. It was like they were doing voodoo over me. Debbie immediately woke me up.

She said, "Carla, I'm leaving, and you need to come with me. You're not safe here. Please come with me."

I replied, "No, you're wrong. I love Henri. He wouldn't do anything to hurt me. I'm good."

She said, "No, you're not. If you don't come with me, I won't come back here for you again."

Once again, I refused to leave. I didn't feel I was in danger. I was in love with Henri and wanted nothing more than to be with him.

Alarmed by my behavior and what she saw, Debbie left and promptly called my mother. She expressed to my mom that she believed I was in extreme danger and needed to be taken out of there. Debbie heard my mother's devastation and knew she feared for my life as well. My mom convinced Debbie to return to

Henri's one more time, but she came with Debbie this time.

I remember I sat in Henri's house and heard a forceful knock on the door. My mother called my name and demanded to see me.

Henri came into the room and said, "You need to come to the door and tell your mother to leave."

Out of my love for him, I obliged. I walked out of the room to tell my mom to leave, but when she saw my appearance, she refused to leave without me.

My hair was messy, my clothes were disheveled, and I had lost a lot of weight. I have vague memories of everything that happened that day. From what I recall, there was shouting, cussing, and accusations back and forth between my mother and Henri. I remember Debbie gathered my belongings while my mother coaxed me to come with her. In the end, I left on one condition that everyone understood I would return in a few days.

Once we left, they took me to the hospital, and they admitted me to the psych ward. My mother spoke to a psychiatrist before her and Debbie came to get me. Based on the information she shared, the psychiatrist told her I might be under the influence of a powerful hallucinogenic drug. The doctor suggested my immediate removal from that environment.

In the hospital, they diagnosed me with severe dehydration and malnourishment, thus the weight loss. I received an IV drip to become hydrated and nourished. During the first few days, I experienced hallucinations. In one of them, I saw Jesus dressed as a police officer, and God spoke to me in the reflection from a light on the ceiling. Those were some helluva hallucinations. I ended up hospitalized for two or three weeks, and my mother left strict instructions that Henri could not visit me under any circumstances.

Once they cleaned my system, the hospital explained there were high levels of PCP in my body.

The doctors said, "If your mother had not gotten you out when she did, you probably would have lost your mind or maybe even died."

I had no idea the good ganga I smoked was actually PCP, better known by its street name, "love boat." PCP was the new rave and must-have drug. Recent news reports described how the drug caused people to become violent, suicidal, and homicidal. Unfortunately, I learned about the dangers of PCP firsthand.

I continued drug counseling and therapy as an outpatient the entire summer upon my release from the hospital. I saw Henri sparingly after that experience. By the time they released me, he had moved his soon-to-be baby mama into his apartment. There wasn't enough room for me, her, and him in the apartment or his life. I had now lost the love of my life and added yet another layer of trauma to my life.

CHAPTER SIX

A few good things came from my experience with Henri, namely, my discovery of and awakening to our rich African heritage. The seed planted by Martin Luther King, Jr.'s assassination had taken root and was being watered. I developed a newfound respect for militant nationalism after learning about the diaspora and social activism.

My eyes were wide open. I no longer wanted to use my "slave" name. I wanted a powerful name indicative of the new me. Someone gave me a book of African names from which I chose Nailah Aisha. The meaning of these two names represented who I was to become. Nailah meant one who succeeds, and Aisha meant life.

I vowed I would succeed at everything I pursued in life. However, it was important to first define what success meant for me. Before my awakening, I thought you had to be rich and famous, like entertainers, athletes, and businessmen, to be successful. I didn't equate success with the everyday people around me. After my awakening, I realized the hardworking people in my family, such as my mother, were, in fact, successful in their own way.

My mother successfully provided for her two daughters as a single parent. Yes, she struggled sometimes, but we never lacked food, clothing, or shelter. Every need was met, and sacrifices were made to ensure we also had some of our wants.

Choosing to be successful and being successful are two different things, and it does not always happen as we envisioned. My plan for success was to return to college and repair my relationship with Artise. However, that was much easier said than done.

I had depression the entire summer, even though I was in therapy. This made me lackadaisical about a return to school. I sincerely wanted to go back, but I could not bring myself to move from my bed. Then, the fall semester of 1978 came, and I again couldn't bring myself to enroll. Instead, I ate, slept, and watched TV the entire semester.

My feelings for Artise and Henri made it difficult for me to choose between them. On the one hand, I still wanted Henri, who clearly did not want me and had moved on with his life. Then there was the Artise that I loved, who also loved and wanted me. It should have been an obvious choice, but it wasn't. For some baffling reason, I pined for the "missed opportunity" with Henri and was unsure if I wanted to move forward with Artise. Ultimately, I chose me and threw myself into school in the spring semester of '79.

Overall, Artise and I were together for six years, and it was a complicated relationship. This was partly because while I professed my love for Artise, I had developed feelings for Henri while Artise was away in the military. Unfortunately, Henri didn't return my feelings, but oddly, that didn't matter. I was the moth to his flame, and I wasn't going down without a fight, even if I was the only one fighting.

Trying to maintain a long-distance relationship at that young age with Artise was difficult. The loneliness we both experienced while separated pushed us to the arms of other lovers. But that's human nature, right?

There's an Isley Brothers song that says, "If you can't be with the one you love, then love the one you're with."

Well, we both took that to heart. Truthfully, I needed to figure out who I was and what I wanted. So, as hard as it was, we decided to take a break. However, we agreed to remain friends. But can you really be friends with someone you had years of history with and still loved?

We enjoyed spending time together as our friendship became like comfort food. Artise was my cozy blanket throughout the many storms I encountered while I worked through my angst. But the one storm he couldn't comfort me through was the news that they planned to station him in South Korea for two years in the fall. To prepare, we vowed to spend as much time together as possible before he had to leave.

For the first time in my life, time literally felt like it flew by like a private jet as summer days passed quickly. Two years not only sounded but felt like forever. Artise could not comfort me since this storm involved him. So, I turned to the temporary warmth of the malfunctioning heated blanket known as Henri. His warmth was of convenience in brief spurts. But honestly, I'm not sure who really used who since I had feelings and he did not. Naturally, this was a time of confusion for me. Here was one man who loved me and one who did not, and I loved them both.

Fall came, and Artise left for South Korea. I thought school would be a great distraction, but shortly after he left, I discovered I was pregnant. One could only imagine the chaos I felt inside because I was unsure who the father was. I tried to track my conception date, but I had slept with both Artise and Henri. To add to my stress, I was not ready for motherhood. However, ready or not, this baby was coming. So, I had to pull myself together and wrap my head around the fact I would be a single mother. My duty was to do everything possible to provide for my baby and myself.

I completed my fall semester of college, and in the middle of the spring semester, March to be exact, my beautiful daughter LaShon Juanita was born. Although Artise was in South Korea and unavailable for a test, Henri agreed to DNA testing. The results came back and confirmed Henri was not the father.

After my daughter's birth, I returned to school and finished the spring semester. At the end of the semester, I enrolled at the Occupational Industrialization Center (OIC), a job training program based in the Mount Pleasant area of DC. The decision to enroll in the OIC was a pivotal moment in my life. I learned the skills needed to become a productive and proficient employee. I graduated from the program in September and took advantage of their job placement assistance. I applied, interviewed, and accepted a clerk-typist position with the District of Columbia Public Schools (DCPS) in November 1980.

CHAPTER
SEVEN

I met some interesting people when I was a student at UDC. One of which was Ms. J. She became my mentor and my daughter's godmother. We both lived at home with our parents, desired something different for our lives, and shared the same views about Pan-Africanism. The idea for us to become roommates came up one day when I visited her. We made plans for how we would share the load and expenses for ourselves and our children. I was all for the idea because it would allow me to leave home and become an independent adult.

Ms. J knew two other women, Ms. W. and Mrs M, who loved the idea of shared housing. Each had their own apartment and had difficulty making ends meet. The four of us met up a few times to discuss the pros and cons of being roommates and what we could expect from the arrangement. We agreed to share all living expenses equitably between the four of us. On an as-needed basis, we would assist each other with childcare. We each would alternate cooking and cleaning the common areas. Lastly, we would be responsible for our individual living spaces.

The next major step was to find housing. Ms. J found a beautiful brownstone on the thirteen hundred block of Euclid Street, NW. It had three levels. The second floor had two bedrooms, one of which had an enclosed side porch and a bathroom. The third floor had two bedrooms and one bathroom. It also had a self-contained one-bedroom basement apartment. It was our dream home.

The four of us and our collective five children moved into the brownstone and called it the Umoja House. At twenty-three years old, I was the youngest of the adults and so excited to move in. My housemates were ten years older than me, and I felt I could learn so much from them.

Ms. J chose the biggest bedroom, which overlooked the front of the house. As a natural hair stylist, she wanted an inviting environment for her clientele as she worked from home. On the third level, Ms. W got the second largest bedroom right above Ms. J. Ms. M selected the basement apartment because she was a fashion designer and needed the extra space.

Between us moms, we had three girls and two boys. They gave two of the girls the room that included the side porch, and the boys took the mid-size bedroom on the third floor. This left the smallest bedroom on the third floor in the back of the house for me and LaShon.

I felt cheated. I was a contributing member of the household and should have received more than leftovers. But I didn't speak up for myself. Instead, I retreated to what was familiar. I returned home to my mother. I told my housemates I was going to spend a few days at my mom's. Well, a few days turned into a few weeks.

My housemates reached out to me because my absence concerned them. The ladies inquired what was going on with me and if I could come by the house to talk with them. I agreed, and it was then that I found the courage to say what was on my mind.

I explained, "As a paying member of the household, I deserve a bigger space than what I have. I know I'm the youngest, but I'm not a kid. I want to be treated like a contributing member."

The ladies heard me out and agreed my concerns were legitimate. I also owned up to the fact I should have told them how I felt sooner. In the end, we decided that the girls and I would switch rooms, and I agreed to let them know when something bothered me from now on. After all, none of us were mind readers.

Life in the Umoja House was better after we cleared the air. It was here that I fully embraced my new name, Nailah. I introduced myself as Nailah to everyone I met. I even told my family to call me Nailah. Naturally, this was hard for my mother. She named me after her biological father, Carl, who died in a house fire six months before my birth. For me to change my name somehow felt like a slap in the face to her. It wasn't just my mother who disagreed with my name change and flat-out refused to call me Nailah. I received pushback from other family members, too. While I understood their viewpoint, I didn't agree with it.

Growing up, I always had issues with my name due to low self-esteem. I felt like I had a boy's name with the letter "a" added to it to make it different. Now that I was older, Nailah better suited me, even though legally, I was still Carla Denise Kennedy.

In the short time we had lived in the Umoja House, LaShon had gotten used to being called Akosua, which was the name I had picked out for her. I realized it sent her mixed signals to be called Akosua most of the time and then LaShon when we were with our family. So, in 1981, shortly after her first birthday, I began the process to legally change both our names to let everyone know I was serious. We became Nailah and Akosua Agyemann.

It was an adjustment for those closest to me to call me Nailah. Initially, I responded when I was called Carla, particularly if it was my mom or someone from her generation. Gradually transitioning them to my new name felt like it might be easier. But for those of my generation, it was different. They were young enough to understand where I was coming from, and for them to continue to refer to me as Carla was a sign of disrespect. Once I explained how I felt disrespected by their refusal to acknowledge my new name, they eventually came around to call me by my legal name.

In May 1981, Artise was discharged from the military. He broke the news to me with a surprise visit to the Umoja House. Although I had sent him pictures of Akosua while he was away, this was the first time he laid eyes on his daughter and held her. I will never forget the look on his face the first time he saw Akosua in person. The tears of joy and love that streamed down his face were something special to behold.

Upon returning home from the military, Artise moved home with his family. However, he spent a lot of time with us so he could get acquainted with Akosua, and we functioned like a family. His first order of business was to find employment. Once he found a job, he spent nights with us since his days were now occupied. This disturbed the peace in the Umoja House.

It was never my intention to cause issues in the Umoja House. I loved it there and the bond between me and the other ladies. But Artise's constant presence apparently broke our code. They brought it to my attention, and it was not pretty. Ms. J came to me without our fellow housemates. She accused me of moving Artise in without discussing it with her and the other housemates.

She said, "What type of games are you playing? You can't just move that man in here like that. You didn't even give us a chance to say yes or no."

I said, "I don't know what you're talking about. Artise does not live here."

She said, "Nailah, he sleeps here, he leaves for work from here, and when he gets off from work, he comes back here!"

I vehemently denied her accusations. The scream fest continued between us, and before I knew it, Ms. J slapped me. I found myself startled and speechless. I had never been much of a fighter, except maybe for fighting my sister growing up. So, I did not hit back, partly out of shock and fear.

When Ms. J told the other housemates about our conversation, she boasted like I was her "bitch" and was afraid of her. This angered me for several reasons. First, I was mad because I did not defend myself, and then I was even angrier because I allowed Ms. J to think she had scared me. I knew it wouldn't be too long before she tried her hand again, but this time, she was in for a rude awakening.

While I don't quite remember the basis for the second altercation, I'm sure it had to do with Artise again. Ms. J and I were in the kitchen, and she slapped me in the middle of our verbal fight. Without hesitation, I punched her in the eye. The look of surprise, bewilderment, and anger was all over her face. She never thought I would hit her back. It was on, and we both began swinging at each other.

Ms. M screamed, "They're fighting," as she ran upstairs to get Artise.

He came downstairs and broke us up by restraining me. I wanted blood. When he finally let me go, I ran upstairs to my bedroom. There, I had stored a five-piece knife set. I ran into the room and grabbed the biggest knife from the set. I came back downstairs, yelling every obscenity I could at Ms. J.

With Artise again restraining me, I said, "Bitch I will fuck you up if you put your hands on me again. I am not scared of you!"

It took a lot for me to calm down that night. I was so heated I even called my mother and told her what happened.

My mom said, "Ms. J must not know you are crazy. She better leave you alone."

Only my mother could get away with that statement, as she referenced my short stay in the psych ward.

Sometime later, we had a house meeting and discussed everything. I listened to my housemates and realized I had inadvertently moved Artise in with me, which was unfair to them. His semi-permanent presence violated what we intended the Umoja House to be. We intended it as a residence for us four women and our children. In hindsight, I should have been more considerate of my housemates as it pertained to Artise and our home.

Now, I was wrong about Artise, but Ms. J was wrong for putting her hands on me.

I argued, "She never would have hit any of you all. She bullied me because I was the youngest. Therefore, the most vulnerable."

I don't remember if she ever apologized, but our relationship was never the same from that day on. After consulting with my mother and stepfather, I left the Umoja House and returned home with Artise. Unfortunately, after I moved back, I no longer stayed in contact with any of the ladies from the Umoja House. I did not have any hard feelings toward Ms. W or Ms. M., but Ms. J, I could do without. In hindsight, my one regret was its impact on Ms. J's relationship with Akosua. My severed friendship with her meant a severed relationship with her goddaughter.

CHAPTER
EIGHT

When I moved back with my mom and stepdad, I wanted to accomplish several goals. After a few months, I saved up enough money to put a down payment on my first car. I purchased a 1976 Ford Valore, and I achieved my first goal. I took a loan through the used car dealership with an outrageously high interest rate because I was so green to the car-buying process. To add to the evidence of my ignorance, the dealer pulled a fast one and only charged the battery enough to drive the car for a few days. I had to buy a new battery shortly after I drove the car off the lot.

As if the battery and interest rate weren't big enough lessons, I soon discovered there was much more to buying a car than meets the eye. I had to register my car for tags and title with the Department of Motor Vehicles (DMV) because of the sketchy dealers I bought it from. I had no clue how to get all this done, but Artise reassured me he would take care of everything. So, I gave him money to pay for the tags.

Artise kept his word and came home with the tags for the car. A friend of mine kept asking me about the title and registration, but I dismissed her. I thought the important part was that the car had tags. Other than her, no one else said anything to me about the need for a title and registration. When I asked Artise about the title and registration, he gave me what I now know was a bogus story, and I believed him. I was so naive.

One night, as I drove through Georgetown with Artise in the passenger seat and Ko asleep in the back, I ran a stop sign. I didn't see the unmarked police car parked nearby, and the next thing I saw was the police lights in my rear-view mirror. I pulled over and rolled down my window for the officer.

He asked, "Ma'am, do you know why I pulled you over?"

I replied, "No, sir."

He said, "You don't? Well, you ran the stop sign back there. Let me see your license and registration."

I said, "I'll give you my license, but I don't have a registration card."

He asked, "Is this your car?"

I said, "Yes."

I handed the officer my license before he walked back to his car. The longer it took the officer to come back to the car, the more antsy Artise became. It was clear at this point that there was more to this registration thing than whatever story Artise told me, and as soon as we got home, I planned to ask him again.

I watched in the side mirror as the officer walked back to my car.

With his hand on his weapon, he said, "Ma'am, you said you own this car?"

I replied, "Yes, I own the car. I just bought it a few weeks ago."

He asked, "Where did you get the tags from?"

I said, "We got them from the DMV."

The officer said, "You couldn't have because these stolen tags belong to another vehicle."

Shocked, I said, "Well, I didn't steal them. My boyfriend said he got them from the DMV."

The officer said, "Is the guy next to you your boyfriend?"

I replied, "Yes."

Immediately, backup was called. Artise was arrested, and the car was impounded. Then, Ko and I were taken to the second district police station. I'm sure you can imagine my level of my pissedivity. I was beyond angry.

I was at level 100 of being pissed off.

I was so humiliated and had to call my mom and stepdad to pick us up. Artise was released later that night after we paid his bail, and believe me, the ride home was not a pleasant one for him. On top of it all, I now had to find money to get the car out of impoundment and properly register and tag it.

The lessons I learned behind that ordeal taught me to take care of important matters myself and, most importantly, educate myself on how to do those important things properly. It was an expensive but valuable lesson learned. Unfortunately, one additional lesson I should have learned was not to trust or believe everything Artise said or did.

Needless to say, my relationship with Artise survived the tag ordeal because I wanted our family to stay intact. I felt we needed to stay together in order to build our future. Not to mention, an addition to our family was on the way. In May 1983, our son Tariq was born, and a year after that, we moved to our first apartment. We found a nice, affordable two-bedroom in Chillum, Maryland.

When we first moved, we did not have much, but what we had was ours. Our home was cozy and comfortable. My bestie, Debbie, visited regularly with her boyfriend, Rob. Ko loved Aunt Debbie's visits because she always brought loads and loads of candy. After the kids went to bed, it was party time for the adults. Debbie and Rob would spend a few hours with us as we watched TV, played cards, smoked weed, and drank alcohol. I really loved our apartment and enjoyed entertaining our friends and family.

Our happy home and high times ended abruptly in February 1985. Crack cocaine ravaged the DC metropolitan area, and unbeknownst to me, Artise had begun smoking it. For months, I gave him my portion of the rent money to add to his to pay the apartment complex. Well, some months, he would partially pay it and tell the leasing office we would pay the rest before the end of the month. This ploy worked for a little while, but then his grace ran out.

One cold February morning, a pink-colored notice slid under the door and stated we were three months behind in rent. We either had to vacate on our own or face eviction later that day. It all came to the light. The money I gave Artise for rent was used to support his crack habit.

I cried hysterically and asked him, "How could you do this to us? I just don't understand."

Artise said nothing. Instead, he silently packed a small bag to leave. I LOST IT! I went to the kitchen and hunted for the biggest knife I could find. I grabbed the knife and came back to the bedroom with the intent of doing him bodily harm. I wanted to stab him right in his heart, but something in me would not allow it. Instead, I pricked him multiple times in the chest with just the tip of the blade.

As he walked out the door, I cut him on the elbow, a scar he carries to this day. I stood in the living room and cried as Ko looked at me for answers while she cried for her daddy. The only one who had peace at that moment was Tariq because he was asleep in his crib.

The only person I could call was my mother. It was seven in the morning, and she had just arrived at work. I explained the eviction and that I needed help. She quickly rallied the troops—Aunts Frances and Regina, my stepdad, Zeke, and his best friend, Mr. Stacy. They arrived with boxes, and we quickly packed my belongings and moved my things out of the apartment. I left everything except the clothes we packed for the kids, myself, and a few other necessities. Artise obviously didn't care about his things other than what he packed in that small bag. So I left his stuff there.

My kids and I became victims of the crack scourge through no fault of our own. We moved back in with my mom and stepdad.

My family said, "We will help you as long as you help yourself. However, if we find out you're taking what we give you to help Artise, we will help you no longer."

I responded, "You do not have to worry about him. I need my family far more than I need him."

Artise walking out on us after he put us in that devastating situation was the proverbial straw that broke the camel's back. At least that's what I thought. The relationship should have swiftly ended due to his actions, but it didn't. We had history.

CHAPTER NINE

I began to pray after I moved back home. I told God I had three goals I wanted to achieve. I wanted a new job, a new car, and a new place for me and my kids. I didn't have any specific order for these goals to be achieved. I just knew I wanted to complete them by my thirtieth birthday, which was in two years.

I got rid of my old Ford Valore when it stopped working. My mother allowed me to use her old car to get the kids and I back and forth to work, school, and daycare. One Friday evening, I had made plans for me and the kids to spend the weekend with Debbie. I was getting ready to leave when my mother told me I couldn't use her car for the weekend. I was furious.

The public bus stopped running at 7:00 pm in our neighborhood and only operated during the morning and evening rush hour. When my mom told me I couldn't use the car, it was almost time for the last bus of the day. The kids and I hurried and made it on the last bus. However, it took two hours for us to get from northwest to southeast DC. That long ride gave me time to think.

I said to myself, "This is the first and last time my mother will snatch her car from me."

I knew I had to get my own car. I just needed to figure out how.

One of my coworkers had a brother who was a car salesman at McLaughlin Oldsmobile. I remembered an article about McLaughlin Oldsmobile being one of a few black-owned car dealerships in the country. It was located on Central Avenue in Princes Georges County, Maryland. When my coworker suggested I visit McLaughlin, it appealed to me because I desired to support black businesses whenever possible.

My trip to McLaughlin did not disappoint. I test-drove an Oldsmobile Firenza, and I loved it. The Firenza was a compact four-door sedan, big enough for my little family. I took the bill of sales to my Credit Union and was approved for the car loan. I did not tell anyone except Debbie my good news. When the time came to pick up the car, she went with me to help get both my new car and mother's car home. I was ecstatic. My first goal was achieved.

I had been employed with DC Public Schools (DCPS) for five years and was assigned to work at a junior high school. The principal, whom I affectionately called "Shorty Bigfoot," ran the school like it was his personal kingdom. Some might say he was passionate about the school, but I think he liked the power and control from being in charge. I experienced his controlling nature and several of his power trips firsthand.

One of my most memorable experiences was the time I had an interview scheduled at another district school. I had applied for a promotion that had been denied to me. I innocently shared the name of the school, the date, and the time of my interview with Shorty Bigfoot. Later, I received a call from the interviewing school that the time and date of the interview had changed. That's when I discovered Shorty Bigfoot had conferred with the interviewing principal and asked him to reschedule my interview. The fact that Shorty Bigfoot could control or persuade the other principal in that manner told me I could not work for him. So, I declined the position.

In Shorty Bigfoot's kingdom, everyone was expected to follow his orders at all costs. If you didn't, there would be hell to pay, but that was too high of a price for me, as he would soon learn. See, Shorty Bigfoot wanted my coworker, Samantha, to resign. He thought if he withheld her paycheck, she would be forced to come into the office and coerce her to resign.

He told the administrative staff to allow everyone except Samantha to come in and pick up her check.

Well, I was out when he gave the royal orders, and when I returned, no one bothered to tell me what had happened. Samantha sent her son to pick up her paycheck, and I gave it to him since I was the only one in the office. Shorty Bigfoot was livid when he found out Samantha had received her check and that I was the one who gave it to her. I grew tired of his belittlement for something I didn't know was an issue. Finally, as I stood before his throne, also known as his desk, and listened to his rant about my stupidity, I decided enough was enough.

For deniability, I bent over his desk to a position where only he could hear me and firmly said, "You can kiss my entire black ass."

The look of shock and disbelief on his face was reward enough for me. I turned, walked out of his office, and left him speechless. Just as I thought, one of my coworkers came to me and mentioned the conversation I had with Shorty Bigfoot.

I looked her dead in the face and flatly said, "I never said anything like that to him," then went on about my business.

Not too long after, I interviewed at another elementary school. This time, I didn't tell anyone at my job about my interview. However, after my references were checked, I didn't get the position. Although I could not prove it, I knew Shorty Bigfoot had bad-mouthed me to the principal during the reference check. I decided it was time to go somewhere he had little to no clout and could not touch me.

The Washington Post newspaper had a column called the Federal Diary, written by Mike Causey. In the column, I read an announcement for a clerk-typist position at a federal government agency in Montgomery County, MD. I called the number listed in the column and scheduled an interview. Although I was born and raised in DC, I rarely traveled to Montgomery County and was unfamiliar with the suburb. I primarily lived, worked, and played in the city and occasionally Prince George's County.

Friday afternoon came, and it was time for my interview. I drove up and down Rockville Pike for at least an hour and could not find the building on Fishers Lane. I accidentally left the news article with the office number at home, so I couldn't stop at a payphone to let them know I was lost. I completely missed the interview and had to wait until Monday morning to explain why I was a no-show.

I called the point of contact listed in the article first thing Monday morning to explain what happened. The person I spoke with was very understanding of my plight.

She said, "I understand. If you're not familiar with the area, you can certainly miss it. For future reference, just know that Fisher Lane is located off Twinbrook Parkway."

As I listened to her, I recalled seeing Twinbrook Parkway as I drove up and down Rockville Pike on Friday. Unfortunately, I didn't get that position. However, they did refer my name to another office for consideration. A couple of days later, I received a call to interview for a clerk-typist position in the agency's Press Office. This time, I was ready.

To prepare, I did a dry run the day before the interview so I would know exactly where to go. On the day of the interview, I arrived fifteen minutes ahead of my scheduled time. Since I kept my hair braided, I wore a suit and one of my mother's curly wigs. I walked confidently into that interview, and I knew I aced it. That position had my name on it, and no one could tell me anything different.

When I received the call from human resources to formally offer the position, I was so excited that everyone in my office heard me accept it. I hung up the phone and immediately went to inform Shorty Bigfoot that Friday would be my last day. Mind you, this took place on a Monday afternoon, which meant I gave him one week's notice.

Perplexed, Shorty Bigfoot said, "I didn't get a call to check your references."

His response gave me all the proof I needed and confirmed his attempts to sabotage my efforts to leave the school.

I proudly responded, "I'm leaving the district

government and going to the federal government. They didn't need to check with you."

His face hit the floor. Checkmate! He had been outsmarted. I beat him at his own game. When Grace, my friend and coworker, heard I submitted my resignation, she immediately took the rest of the day off. That afternoon, she went to her part-time job at a local grocery store and told them she desired to come back as a full-time employee.

See, Shorty Bigfoot not only used his position for power and control. He also used it to obtain sexual favors from women willing to play his game to get ahead. I was not one of those women. He tried his hand, but I refused and often acted as a buffer for Grace against his advances. I felt, and still feel, that I'd rather succeed in my career by my merits than be a slave to sexual favors to get ahead.

I became an employee of the Press Office in September 1986, and my goal of a new job was achieved. It was a culture shock for me because I shifted from an all-black environment to being the only black person and black woman in the office. It was my responsibility to clip all articles that mentioned the agency. I then made copies of the articles and arranged them into packets for distribution to the agency's senior-level leadership. This was called the Daily Press Clippings. I enjoyed this part of the job because it allowed me time to get to know other people in the organization.

One day I spotted a tall, dark, and handsome man as he stepped off the elevator and walked very quickly.

I thought to myself, "Who is that?"

He was HOT. Of course, I didn't have the nerve to approach him. So, I only observed him from afar. Imagine my surprise when I found out he worked in a different branch of the press office.

One day, he came to see the administrative officer (AO) who worked in my office. The AO called me into her office and introduced us. I formally met "Mister" on a beautiful fall October day, and a flame was ignited.

CHAPTER TEN

Things at my new job were going well, but life at home turned upside down. My mom and Zeke decided to go their separate ways. On top of that, the owners of the rental house asked them to vacate. This meant the kids and I needed a place to stay.

My mother found a one-bedroom apartment to live in, but it was too small to accommodate me and the kids, even for a short period of time. The saving grace came through my aunt Regina, who had a townhouse in Landover, Maryland. She lived alone and invited us to move in with her.

Moving in with Aunt Regina provided the clean break I needed from Artise. As I stated earlier, we had history, and it was sometimes hard to ignore the good and the bad. After we separated, Artise moved to a small apartment on Quincy Place in Northwest DC.

We agreed the kids would spend time with him there every weekend. He occasionally asked me to stay over as well, and I obliged. This naturally confused Ko as she thought Mommy and Daddy were back together. Tariq was only three years old and too young to understand.

Artise gave up his Quincy Place apartment and moved into the basement apartment of one of his friends, who lived a few doors away from us on Tuckerman Street. That relational history was hard to navigate during our breakup, which sometimes complicated things with my parents.

When I had a male friend visit me, my mother asked, "Why would you go out with someone else when Artise lives nearby."

Artise felt like I betrayed him. The whole situation was so complicated.

When I finally moved from Tuckerman Street to Landover with Aunt Regina, I cut all communication and ties with Artise and his family. I needed to heal from the trauma and hurt inflicted by him. He did not know where I lived, worked or how to contact me. I needed this space to build my little family. I assured my children that no matter what, we would always have each other, and we would be there for one another always.

Aunt Regina helped me find before and after-school care for Ko, who was in the first grade. Then, I found a daycare through a childcare assistance program for Tariq near my job. With my home life settled, I focused on the new job.

At work, Mister introduced me to the coworkers in his office. He also introduced me to other black employees in the organization. These introductions helped me adjust to my new work environment.

Mister had an office in his department, and I found myself there a lot. I loved to be around people who made me feel comfortable and looked like me. One of the ladies I met was Ms. S. I enjoyed laughing and joking with her. She had a dry wit and was knowledgeable about the press office. Occasionally, Mister and I would eat lunch together outside of the office. This was his way of showing me the surrounding area, which I appreciated.

One day in November, Mister didn't come to work, and I realized I missed him tremendously. We went out to lunch when he returned to the office.

He asked, "So, did you miss me?"

Puzzled that he even asked, I didn't know how to respond. My insides fluttered like a little schoolgirl who just found out her secret crush knew her name.

He must have read my mind because he said, "It's okay if you did. I missed you too."

After I heard his response, I admitted, "Well, I did miss you a little."

He chuckled and casually said, "Yeah, I had to take my wife out of town."

His wife! What the entire hell? Who knew he had a

wife? He had never said anything about a wife before. Where was his ring? What type of games was he playing with me? I assumed he was single with all the time we spent together at work—foolish me. At 29, I still had so much to learn about men.

At that precise moment, he was no longer fair game to me. He was a married man, and I was not about to break my cardinal rule, which was never to get involved with a married man. I didn't want another woman to do that to me, so I wasn't going to do it to anyone else.

Our friendship continued to flourish, although there was no hope for a romantic relationship. I knew exactly where he stood in my life—squarely in the friend zone. One day, I locked my keys in the car, still in the ignition, and needed a ride home to obtain the spare.

Mister said, "I'll give you a ride home to get your keys after work, and then I'll bring you back to your car."

Remember now, I lived in Landover, he lived on Capitol Hill, and our job was in Rockville. This is a ninety-minute commute one way in rush hour traffic. We left work and stopped by Twinbrook Metro Subway Station to pick up his wife before we continued to my house. The way Mister greeted his wife was my reinforcement that we were just friends. We got to my house, he dropped me off and took his wife home. True to his word, he came back later in the evening and drove me back to my car.

I must admit, it was nice to have the attention of a TDH (tall, dark, and handsome) man. Our daily chats included every aspect of our lives. He even expressed interest in meeting my kids because I talked about them constantly. His genuine interest made me feel like he was indeed concerned about my well-being as his friend.

One Friday evening, Mister called me unexpectedly. I had just put the kids to bed and was watching TV.

He said, "What you doing?"

I said, "Nothing but watching TV."

He said, "Well, how about I come over and watch TV with you?"

Intrigued about the real nature of this call, I said, "Sure. That's what friends do, watch TV together on a Friday night, right?"

So, he came over, and we watched TV for a while. Then, Mister said he was hungry and wanted to grab something to eat. He invited me to go with him, and we ended up at Denny's. After we finished eating, neither of us wanted the night to end. I suggested we go to Hains Point, but that was vetoed as it was December and too cold to sit on the waterfront. Mister suggested we go to a hotel to escape the cold night air.

I said, "Okay."

When we got into the hotel room, Mister completely stripped his clothes off and got in the bed. He didn't ask me to join him. However, I laid down beside him, completely dressed in my sweat suit on top of the covers. Lying beside him increased the flame that ignited the first day I saw him to a five-alarm fire. It consumed me so much that I wanted to feel his naked body next to mine. Before I realized it, I had stripped and slipped under the covers with him. I broke my cardinal rule.

Based on my previous sexual experiences, I thought all I had to do was lay there and let the man do all the work. So, I laid there and let him have his way. I did not move one inch. I could feel him slowly moving my body to his rhythm, so I began to move with him. I got so into it I found myself reenacting a scene from a movie I once saw. That night, I felt like I had become a woman for the first time in my life.

Monday came, and we returned to work. Mister came to my office to see me.

He said, "I thought about you all weekend. You trying to make me leave my wife?"

I replied, "No, because if you leave your wife for me, you'll leave me for someone else."

He said, "How do you feel about being my mistress?"

Being the green and naïve person I was, I asked, "What is a mistress?"

He went on to explain that since he was a married man, he wouldn't be able to see me often after work. So, to make up for the lack of time, he would give me money or do things for me that I could not do for myself.

Appalled by his explanation, I said, "That sounds like a prostitute to me. If I want to give you some, I'll do it for free."

Looking back, I'm sure my response was music to Mister's ears. If only I knew then what I know now.

CHAPTER
ELEVEN

It was Christmas time, and this was me and the kids' first Christmas since moving in with Regina. Ko was now six, and Tariq was three. Regina was excited to have little people in the house. She went overboard to ensure the kids had a great Christmas. Aunt Frances was excited too. She came to spend the night with us on Christmas Eve. She wanted to see the kids' faces on Christmas morning.

Right before I put them to bed, Tariq said, "Mommy, we don't have a chimney for Santa to come down. How is he going to get in the house?"

I said, "Well, Santa will ring the doorbell. But he's not going to come unless you guys are sleeping."

Shortly after putting them to bed, the doorbell rang as if on cue. To my surprise, on the other side of the door stood Mister.

He said, "I came to help put the kids' toys together."

Imagine my delight at this unexpected treat. Without missing a beat, Tariq, followed by Ko, came upstairs to see Santa, who had rung the doorbell. To their disappointment, it was not Santa. However, I introduced them to Mister for the first time. Although the kids weren't initially excited to meet him, he earned brownie points with my aunts because he showed up and helped me put their toys together.

Mister made sure he stayed until after midnight. Later, he told me he did that so I wouldn't be alone on Christmas day. In one of our previous conversations, I mentioned that I dreaded time with my family on Christmas day because, unlike my sister and cousins, I was not married or in a committed relationship. That Christmas, I fell hard for Mister.

The clandestine nature of me and Mister's relationship was fun. As a TDH man, there were plenty of women who desired him. I know because they told me so. They had no idea of the true nature of our friendship. One woman often told me all the ways she tried to entice Mister to come to her place, but he would always say no.

It made me laugh inwardly to know he and I were together and other women were clueless. Keep in mind, these were beautiful, stylish, competent, and successful women that pursued him. By comparison, I was very simple. I did not wear the latest and greatest fashions or a lot of make-up. It was never my thing to keep up with the latest fashion designer handbags and clothes. I dressed well and looked good in my clothes, but I didn't need a high price tag to do it. Besides, I was a single parent. My first priority was ensuring my kids had everything they needed. The relationship with Mister grew and continued far longer than I ever imagined.

A few years prior, I had applied for the Section 8 housing program in DC and was placed on the waitlist. I was on this list for years, and the last time I checked, I was number forty on the list. One morning, my phone rang, and it was Aunt Regina. Strangely, she asked for my social security number. I complied and gave her the requested information even though I was confused.

In June, I received a letter that stated my name had moved to the number one slot, and I had sixty days to find affordable housing. To add to this great news, I could now use the new Section 8 housing voucher, which allowed it to be used anywhere in the country. When I first applied for Section 8, one of the conditions of the program was that I reside in DC. With the limits taken off, the entire Washington, DC Metro area was my oyster. This was the opportunity I needed to move closer to work.

I immediately began a search for housing in Montgomery County, MD. If I moved closer to the job, it would reduce my two-hour daily commute. The apartment search was harder than I thought. Thankfully, my knight in shining armor, Mister, came to the rescue. He told me about the Housing Opportunity Commission (HOC) and how they could assist me with my search.

I contacted the HOC, and they were a great help. They gave me a list of affordable housing in Montgomery County. Then, they helped me move my housing voucher and case from DC to the county. They also informed me the law required a three-bedroom apartment because my children were of the opposite sex.

Mister joined me on the apartment hunt during lunch because I didn't know my way around the area. This was before Mapquest, Google Maps, and Waze. Back then, you were helpless if you didn't know where you were going or how to use a fold-up map. Eventually, I fell in love with an apartment in Takoma Park.

The apartment had a very spacious living room, nice-sized dining room and kitchen, and three spacious bedrooms. There was a full bathroom in the main bedroom and hardwood floors throughout the entire apartment. The move to Takoma Park shortened my commute to exactly sixty minutes roundtrip. There were a few drawbacks. The unit was on the first floor, which meant the bedroom windows were at ground level. It didn't have central air and heating and no onsite laundry facility. Despite the amenities it lacked, I applied for the apartment and got approved before my sixty-day deadline.

While I searched for an apartment, the timing belt broke on my beloved "Bitsy," my car, and she had to be put in the shop. I had already saved enough money for the first month's rent, the security deposit, and extra funds to cover the moving expenses. The broken timing belt meant that I would need to pull from my moving fund to get my car fixed.

I told my sister Karen about my dilemma, and she suggested I ask Aunt Regina for the money, but I flatly refused. Regina had already done so much for me, and I couldn't bring myself to ask her for the money. I couldn't decide what to do. I wanted my apartment and my car fixed but simply did not have the means to do both.

Mister picked me up every morning, took me to work, and brought me back home in the evening while my car was in the shop. Yes, he embarked on the ninety-minute commute from Capitol Hill to Landover to Rockville to Landover and then back to Capitol Hill. How could I not love that man?

One day, as Mister dropped me off after work, it shocked me as my car sat in the parking lot.

I was so surprised and yelled out loud, "My car!"

Immediately, I knew Aunt Regina was the one who got my car fixed. I jumped out of Mister's car and ran inside the house. I hugged Regina as tears flowed from my eyes and thanked her for what she had done. Later that evening, she recounted her conversation with Karen.

She said, "I knew you would not ask her for the money. So, I decided to take matters into my own hands. Now, are you sure you're ready to live on your own?"

I said, "No. But I feel like if I don't move now, I will never move."

She hugged me and said, "I understand exactly what you're saying, and I support your decision."

Now that I had the car situation behind me, I was ready to move forward and relocate to my new apartment. On August 25, 1987, the kids and I moved to Houston Avenue, Takoma Park, MD. It was four days before my 30th birthday, and just like that, I had achieved all three goals within two years. I didn't understand it at the time, but God blessed me in my mess.

CHAPTER TWELVE

Mister once told me I got the position in the agency because my new office faced a racial discrimination lawsuit and needed to show diversity. So, I was hired to fill two quotas—a black person and a woman.

I vehemently disagreed with him and said, "I got this job because I was the best-qualified candidate."

To which he said, "Ok. Well, if you don't get promoted on your one-year anniversary, do not stay in that office."

My one-year anniversary came shortly after the move into my Takoma Park apartment. Needless to say, I was a little preoccupied. However, I did manage to find time and ask about my promotion, and just as Mister predicted, I was denied. Their justification was they did not have the slot to promote me.

Now, the young white woman, whose position I

filled when she left, decided she did not like the private sector as much as she thought. So, she was rehired but in the position that would have been my promotion. What a slap in the face! While I could not prove any of this, the optics were there. When I came into the federal government, I took a four thousand dollar annual cut in pay. Don't get me wrong, it was worth it to get away from Shorty Bigfoot. However, now that I lived on my own, I needed more income to meet my increased expenses. Back to the job hunt I went.

In those days, the application process was not centralized like it is now. Back then, an application had to be submitted to each individual human resource office in person. I needed a promotion, so one day, I took copies of my resume and dropped them off at seventeen HR offices. I was on the hunt for a GS-5 position. I applied to those with and without promotion potential and anything I thought I qualified for. Even if the announcement was for a GS-4 Clerk Typist with the potential of a GS-5 Secretary, I applied. If the position was a straight GS-5 with no promotion potential, I applied.

I received two interview requests within the same agency but in different departments. I interviewed for a procurement assistant position within the contract office and an administrative position within a research office. The interview went well for the contract office, and a few days later, I received an unofficial call from the contracting officer stating I had been selected for the position. However, I had to wait for the official call from HR to confirm I had been selected.

In the meantime, I interviewed for the administrative assistant position in the research office and was offered the job almost immediately. But there was a fly in the ointment. When HR called to offer the admin position, they offered me the GS-4 Clerk-Typist. I knew I couldn't take the position at the GS-4 level because it wouldn't provide the pay increase I needed. So, I took a leap of faith and counter-offered.

I said, "If the job is offered at the GS-5 Secretary level, I will accept it."

I could hear the anguished sigh from the HR rep as she hung up. However, the next day, she called back and offered the position at the GS-5 level, and I readily accepted. I left the Press Office in late December and became a GS-5 Clerk-Typist.

Once I started my new position, I called the Contract Officer about the position I had interviewed for with them and inquired if they were still interested in hiring me.

The representative responded, "Yes."

I said, "Well, I never received the official call from HR. So, I accepted a position with another department within your agency at the GS-5 level. With that being said, I cannot accept the lower grade position."

When the HR representative for the contract office finally called to offer the position, it was explained to me that I would have to accept a downgrade to the GS-4 because I didn't have enough experience for their GS-5 position. However, they would bring me on at the GS-4 level but allow me to keep the GS-5 salary. That sounded like a fair deal to me. Now, I would finally be able to recoup the four thousand dollars I lost when I initially transitioned to the government from the public school system.

The HR office called my current supervisor to coordinate my transfer within the new agency. I heard the scream from the executive assistant's office when she received the call that I would be relocated to procurement. She and I were the only support staff the director had. In the two weeks I worked there, she had gotten used to delegating tasks to me. Now, she only had two more weeks of my help before I left for my new position in the contract office. I worked as an administrative assistant for a total of four weeks. Although I didn't recognize it then, God's hand was all over my work situation.

In early January 1988, I became the procurement assistant for the contracting officer and three contract specialists. I assisted them in processing contracts that procured services and goods for the agency. The office was fast-paced, particularly during the fourth quarter of the fiscal year when all the contract monies had to be awarded. The frenzy in the office during that time could be nerve-racking, especially for those unfamiliar with the process. I was blessed to join the office in the second quarter of the fiscal year when it wasn't too busy.

As the fiscal and calendar year progressed, the hectic pace of the office increased. Fortunately, the contracting officer and contract specialists walked me through what they needed from me and what the finished product should look like. Their reasoning was if they explained their expectations to me up front, there would be less margin for errors. Now, no one is perfect, not even me, though sometimes I like to think I am. But the way I was trained worked perfectly. I met all the deadlines, and most of my finished documents were flawless. Life at work was as good as could be expected.

CHAPTER
THIRTEEN

My relationship with Mister became more intense as time passed. Having my own place gave us more opportunities to be together regularly, and it gave him and my kids time to get to know each other better. This arrangement became a conflict. The more I was with him, the more I wanted to be his and he mine. But he was still a married man. Being with him was playing with fire, but I didn't care. My love for him blinded me. I was so blind and naïve that I didn't see the signs of the womanizer in him.

Sexually, I became a woman with this man. Under his tutelage, I learned to be sensual and that I deserved to receive as well as give pleasure. It was not lust. It was passion. It was not just sex it was love. The floodgates of my heart, soul, and body were open for him. I was his queen and secure in my relationship with him until I wasn't.

I decided not to date anyone else and give myself exclusively to Mister. I made this decision because I knew I was the only woman he was involved with outside of his wife. As fate would have it, I learned the devastating truth about Mister.

Mister and I were attending a major business conference held annually in August. The conference was in Missouri. We each went as delegates for our respective work chapters. I thought this was the perfect opportunity for us to spend time together out of town. Unfortunately, he had other plans.

I bumped into Mister at the airport. I was genuinely surprised to see him and didn't know we were on the same flight. He, on the other hand, seemed a little jumpy and dismissive of me. I quickly found out why. Apparently, he was with his girlfriend, Ms. Thang. Although they were undercover, he did not mind being seen publicly with her.

They thought if another man hung out with them on their outings, people wouldn't suspect they were seeing each other. But my gut told me something different, and it crushed me. However, I refused to allow him or them to put a damper on my trip. I met up with my friends and had a fantastic week in St. Louis.

Upon our return home, I asked Mister about Ms. Thang.

He explained, "Babe, she's just a colleague, and there is nothing but a friendship."

Yeah right. But despite my suspicions, I did not stop seeing Mister. After all, I was in love with him.

Over the next three years, things began to change. Mister and his wife divorced, and there was more evidence that he and Ms. Thang were a couple. As usual, I accepted his explanations and ignored the signs and my gut. My eye was on the prize of him finally being all mine, and I didn't have time to entertain anything contrary. That is until the day I found Ms. Thang's phone number in his cell phone. Yes, I snooped through his phone. The old folks say, "Seek, and you will find." Well, I sought, and I found. Although, I am not proud of what I did next.

I wrote down Ms. Thang's number and took it to work with me the next day. Then, I called Ms. Thang at work.

I said, "Bitch, leave my man alone."

Immediately, I felt remorse. First, I had no clue whether she knew about me. Secondly, my anger was not with her. It was with him, but I feared losing him. So, I didn't want to confront him about her with all the fury I felt. Therefore, she got the brunt of my anger. Lastly, I called her on a federal phone, and she felt threatened by my actions. In which case, she had every right to pursue felony charges against me.

Mister was at my house when he received the call from Ms. Thang, who informed him that I called and threatened her. Immediately, he left to go calm and console her, which pissed me off even more. According to him, she planned to press charges against me, but he convinced her not to go through with it.

He explained, "I told her you were a single parent, and if you get arrested, there would be no one to take care of your young kids."

He saved my skin that day, and despite all that I knew, there was no way I would give up my spot in his life easily. After all, I had spent the past six years of my life building this thing we had.

Four years after seeing Ms Thang with Mister in St. Louis, I noticed her at the annual conference in Atlanta. I walked up to her, introduced myself, and apologized.

I expressed, "I'm sorry for taking my anger out on you that day. You might not have known about me, but he certainly did. But do you know we're still seeing each other and sleeping together?"

To prove this to her, we walked to my hotel room and called him, allowing her to hear the conversation. We then came up with the idea to call him out in public later that night.

She said, "Mister and I are going to a jazz club tonight. You should walk past our table and confront him right there in front of everyone."

It sounded like the perfect revenge to me.

As planned, things went off without a hitch. I was a little scared at the beginning of my tirade, but the more I said, the more emboldened I became. In the end, I said everything I had been afraid to say to him, and it felt good. The look on his face was priceless as I aired our dirty laundry, and he tried to defend himself. At that moment, I did not care that I was embarrassing myself. As far as I was concerned, I would never see most of those people ever again. And so what if I did?

The next morning, I felt apprehensive, much like buyer's remorse. I thought about how angry Mister probably was with me. I knew we needed time and space. I hoped the time apart would be enough for his anger to subside.

After I returned home from Atlanta, a good friend invited me to visit her church one Sunday. I was so numb, hurt, and sorrowful. I felt nothing but pain as I sat on that pew. I don't even recall hearing the sermon. My soul was in anguish and felt inconsolable.

When I got home from church, I self-medicated by smoking weed.

As I stood in the bathroom, a voice said, "Seek Jesus."

I repeated out loud, "Seek Jesus?"

The voice said, "Yes."

The voice I heard sounded like it was underwater. So, I pulled back the shower curtain to see if anyone was there, but there was not. Immediately, I dismissed what I heard and thought I was tripping. Little did I know that was the first time the Holy Spirit spoke to me.

I called Mister at work after a few weeks had passed. When he answered, I made up the excuse that I wanted one of his tape cassettes. That was the only lame excuse I could come up with to see him. He was still upset but agreed to let me come to his place to get it.

When I arrived, I could tell that his anger had subsided. We talked about what happened.

He said, "You know Ms. Thang played you, right? She asked me to stop seeing you, but I told her no."

I didn't care one bit that she thought she played me, but I felt some kind of way about her asking him to end our relationship. Oddly enough, I ran into her in a department store many years later. She didn't recognize me until I mentioned Mister. She called him a dog and confirmed that he refused her request to stop seeing me.

Now, back to that night at Mister's. He asked me to leave after our conversation was over. I sat outside his place in the car and cried my eyes and heart out. Then I heard him tap on my window with the most empathic look in his eyes.

He said, "Come back inside."

Mister consoled and comforted me when he took me in his arms. He apologized for his actions that led to the scene in Atlanta and for the hurt he caused me. Then we made passionate love on his sofa.

After such passionate lovemaking, I thought for sure Ms Thang was in his rear-view mirror. How wrong was I? I was in a love triangle as Mister continued to see us both. I can't blame anyone but myself for my continued involvement with him. I loved him unquestioningly with all I had for many years.

The years I spent with Mister were filled with good and bad times. When I totaled my car and did not have transportation for a few months, he let me use his car to run errands. When I needed a male's perspective on how to raise my son when he acted out, he allowed my child to spend the night and bond with him. His influence in my son's life was welcomed and needed—moments like those helped endear him to my heart. However, the terrible moments with Mister pushed me to medicate my hurt and take my anger out on those that I loved the most: my kids.

My mother's discipline hurt me physically and emotionally when I was a child. The physical pain inflicted by the belt, extension cord, or whatever she could get her hands on, coupled with feelings of being unloved, was a lot. Since I could not tell my mother how I felt, I would cry and suffer in silence.

Sometimes, my sister was the unfortunate recipient of my anger towards my mother. I knew I couldn't fight my mother, so I fought with my sister instead. I figured as the oldest child, it entitled me to the upper hand when we fought. That was until my mother gave Karen some advice.

She told Karen, "If you stop fighting Carla like she is your sister and fight her like your enemy, you can beat her."

Why did my mother tell her that?! With her newfound insight, the last time we fought, she kicked my butt.

Just as with my mother, when Mister hurt me, I also cried and suffered in silence. I felt like I didn't have a voice to express how I really felt. When the emotional pain turned to anger, my children received the brunt of it. I didn't realize what I was doing until one night at the dinner table, my son confronted me.

He said, "Mommy, you don't beat us. You beat us up."

He was about ten or eleven years old. At that moment, I realized I had become an abusive parent. I transferred my anger at Mister to those most vulnerable in my life. My intentions were never to abuse my kids, but I did not know how to deal with my emotions and pain. I followed the example my parents set for me, but I forgot how it made me feel to be a receiver of their emotional, mental, and physical pain.

One would think the revelation would have empowered me to change and redirect my anger to the person it belonged to, but it did not. My fear of losing Mister was greater than the feeling of empowerment.

So, steeped in my fear, I continued to believe I was powerless and voiceless.

In my head, I cussed Mister out royally and threw verbal punches all over his body. But in reality, the words just never seemed to come out. Instead, I continued with the status quo and gave him the power in the relationship.

I drank, drugged, and sexed the pain away. During this time, my preferred drug of choice switched from weed to cocaine. Coke numbed the pain far greater than weed. Not to mention weed enhanced my libido, so I did not need to be horny for him when I was angry at him. How does one leave a toxic relationship when they feel powerless? One cannot do so in their own effort. It takes strength they rarely possess.

CHAPTER
FOURTEEN

God allows situations and circumstances to get our attention. We often don't recognize or realize when He taps on our shoulders. One such instance occurred to me on Thursday, August 13, 1998.

Tariq was fifteen years old. He came home intoxicated the night before. His behavior was so out of control that I wouldn't allow him to stay in the house while Akosua and I were at work. Per our routine, I woke him up so he could prepare to leave for the day.

Still hung over, he said, "I don't have anywhere to go."

I responded, "I don't care where you go as long as you leave my house."

We were in the kitchen yelling back and forth at each other. He was adamant about not leaving, and I was just as adamant that he must go. I opened the silverware drawer and took out the eight-inch butcher knife.

I thought to myself, "I should throw this."

No sooner than the thought entered my mind, I threw the knife. Tariq turned his body as he saw the knife coming towards him. The blade penetrated three inches into his lower back.

Akosua screamed, "Mommy, what did you do?"

Tariq writhed with pain in the corner. As soon as I threw the knife, I regretted it and called 9-1-1 while crying.

In my hysteria, I told the dispatcher that I stabbed my son. They dispatched police and an ambulance to my home. The ambulance transported Tariq to the hospital, and they carried me away by the police cruiser. I felt so humiliated as my neighbors watched me drive away in handcuffs.

I remained handcuffed to a chair at the police station while they took my statement. I was there for what seemed like hours before they escorted me to a holding cell. The closing of the cell door jarred me because it felt so unreal.

I thought, "I don't belong here. This is a big mistake. When will this get sorted out so I can go home?"

I was told I had to go in front of a commissioner who would determine what charges they would bring against me. The even bigger kicker was that I had to wait until the next day to see the commissioner. In the meantime, they allowed me one phone call, and I contacted the only person I trusted to help me, Mister.

I told Mister everything and asked him to check on Ko and Tariq.

He said, "Don't worry. Everything will be fine."

Now, how could I not worry? I had no information about Tariq's injury or my fate.

As part of the intake process, I met with a psychologist.

The psychologist asked, "How are you feeling? Do you have any thoughts of suicide?"

I responded, "Not too great. I don't know how my kids are doing, and I don't know when I'll be able to get out of here. But no, I'm not having any thoughts of suicide."

In my cell that night, I prayed and asked God to take care of me and my kids. I knew there were some lessons in this for me to learn, but at the time, I didn't know what they were.

They held my arraignment the next morning. The court broadcasted my hearing from the jail to the courtroom. My mother, Aunts Frances and Regina, and my friends, Ms. G and Ms. V, watched and waited for the prosecutor to reveal my fate. They charged me with attempted murder of a juvenile, child abuse, and child endangerment. These were felony charges and carried a total sentence of seventy years. They held me without bond, which meant I could not return home. I was stunned.

The unfamiliar jail environment was inhospitable in the beginning. I didn't know anyone, so my first loyalty was to myself. However, it was not so bad after I got to know the women in the general population (gen-pop). Like me, they were women with problems, lives, and situations. I even found a familiar face among the women. I knew her from when she used to date one of Artise's friends. Running into her made confinement bearable.

One time, while in the recreation yard, I made a comment that upset another woman. She got all up in my face and yelled. I looked straight ahead because I did not want to be placed in solitary confinement for fighting. I shook in my shoes, but I could not show fear. Never show fear. That's something I learned from my observations and talks with the other women. Later that afternoon, another woman expressed her admiration for my strength in not being scared at that moment. If she only knew how scared I really was.

Since the charges against me involved a minor, Children Protective Service got involved. They sent someone to visit me in jail.

When I met the representative, my first question to him was, "What is going to happen to my son?"

He said, "You do not belong here. You are a mother; your first concern was for your son."

After he completed the interview, he asked, "Do you have an attorney?"

"No," I responded.

He provided me with Mr. Huff's name and number and instructed me to mention him as the referral. I contacted Mr. Huff as soon as I could, and he agreed to represent me.

While I waited for Mr. Huff to do his job in the courtroom, I enrolled in the Montgomery College program at the jail. I took a psychology class that helped me understand how and why I ended up in this situation. I enjoyed the course and was grateful for the enlightenment.

I celebrated my forty-first birthday locked up. The morning mail call had a slew of birthday cards from family and friends. That made me feel so loved and special. When I woke up from my nap later that day, the women surprised me by singing Happy Birthday, Stevie's version. They made a huge birthday card signed by everyone in our cell block. The cherry on top of the proverbial sundae was our fried chicken dinner and a yellow cake with chocolate icing for dessert. I felt like God smiled on me that day because they were both some of my favorite foods.

A few days after my birthday, Mr. Huff informed me a court date was set to argue for my release. The hearing was scheduled for Friday, September 4th, which was the start of the Labor Day weekend. They transported me and the other inmates scheduled for court that day from the jail at 5:00 am. Mr. Huff successfully argued my case, and the judge ordered my release. Since Monday was a holiday, I had to be released that day. Otherwise, I had to wait until Tuesday.

I arrived back at the jail at about noon. I missed lunch, but I didn't care. I was finally going home. I began to pack my belongings and gave away the things I could or did not want to take with me. Then, I waited and waited and waited. I was not released until 9:00 pm. When I walked out of those gates, I was so happy to see Ms. G and Ms. V waiting to take me home.

The first place I wanted to go to was Popeye's Chicken for something to eat. I was hungry because I missed lunch, and dinner was not prepared for me due to my scheduled release. I called my mother while en route to let her know I was released and on my way home. I called Mister once I arrived home. No one told him I had been released, but he was happy to hear I was home. Finally, I was in my own bed, and it was the best night's rest in three weeks.

The next day, I hung out with my friend Ms. K., and she asked me to take a ride with her. We smoked a couple of joints while in the car, and I did not think anything of it. I wanted to have fun and celebrate being home. Well, the following Tuesday, I had my first appointment with Pretrial Services, which was one of the conditions of my release. I had no idea a urine test was required for drugs and alcohol. The test result came back positive for marijuana.

In the interview, they informed me that my release

prohibited weed and alcohol. No alcohol was easy for me because it was not my preferred vice. But it was hard to resist smoking weed. I researched and found that the body stores weed in the fat cells for fourteen days. However, cocaine stays in the body for three days, so cocaine became my drug of choice.

My job placed me on paid administrative leave pending the outcome of my court trial, which was scheduled for mid-October. Depression and worry consumed me. I was worried about whether I would go to jail. It depressed me not to work, not see or talk to Tariq, randomly pee in a cup, and not know what lay ahead for me. The more depressed I became, the more coke I used.

Snorting coke by yourself is not the thing to do when you're depressed. Yet, I did it constantly. I ate, slept, and did coke almost every day because I thought I was smarter than the system. I went to the pretrial service office on Tuesday afternoons. As soon as I returned home, I snorted coke from Tuesday evening through late Friday night. I drank a detox concoction to flush my system Saturday through Monday. My plan worked like a charm. Or so I thought.

As my court date approached, I became even more anxious about the outcome. I was quite irritable because I didn't know what to expect. A few days before the trial date, I asked my family not to come to the courtroom. The morning of the trial, I spoke with my mother, who really wanted to be there. Still, I was adamant about her and other family members not to attend the trial. I just didn't want my family there if I was sentenced to prison. I faced seventy years and did not want them to see me get that much time. The only people I allowed to attend were Ms. V and Ms. G.

I was so nervous when I arrived for the trial at the District Court of Montgomery County in Rockville, MD. My Aunt Frances and Aunt Regina sat in the courtroom. I must admit I was happy to see them, but at the same time, I felt bad because I told my mother not to come. My aunts came to support me despite my request for them not to come. They knew I needed family support, and the judge needed to see that I had a family present.

I sat calmly and listened to the prosecutor outline his case against me; all the while, I cried inside. Tears fell from my eyes as the recording of the 9-1-1 call from the day of the incident played in the courtroom. I bowed my head to conceal my tears from the onlookers in the courtroom. Hearing myself say that I stabbed my son was more than I could bear. This was the crux of the prosecution's case against me and the reason I was charged with attempted murder. My own words put me on trial. His final blow was more damaging. My last drug test came back positive for cocaine use. On this, the prosecutor rested his case.

Then, it was time for Mr. Huff to present my defense. He argued I was a single parent and had done my best to raise a young man who challenged my authority. He further argued that I had lived for forty years as a law-abiding citizen, been gainfully employed for eighteen years, and had been a productive citizen and resident of the county for eleven years without any incidents. Lastly, Mr. Huff argued that since this was my first incident with the criminal system, I should not be locked away for seventy years. Instead, the charges against me should be reduced from felonies to misdemeanors.

The trial was without a jury, so the judge had the final say. Her words made me feel like she saw and understood me.

She said, "As a single mother, I understand how hard it is to raise children alone. I understand that after working eight hours, Ms. Agyemann's work is not over. When she gets home, she has more work to do parenting her children, and there is no cutoff time for this job. I felt your remorse as I watched your tears while the 9-1-1 recording was played. And your counsel is correct. You do not deserve the time the prosecution is recommending. Therefore, I am reducing the felony charges to misdemeanors, and I am giving you two years of probation to include random drug and alcohol testing. Furthermore, you will be placed on the child abuse registry for ten years. You and your son are hereby required to attend individual therapy sessions. If you stay out of trouble with no further infractions for the next two years, I will expunge your case altogether."

I broke down in tears of relief. I was not going back to jail. That alone was an indescribable feeling.

I returned to work within days of my trial. On my first day back, a meeting was held with a Human Resources representative, my supervisor, the assistant branch chief, and the branch chief. The details of the meeting are blurry, but I remember they depicted me as aggressive, angry, and difficult to work with. Then, my work ethic was called into question. That was all a bunch of bull, in my opinion.

Prior to my arrest and being placed on administrative leave, I had not received any negative feedback about my performance at annual or mid-year evaluations. In fact, I regularly received outstanding performance ratings and cash awards for those ratings. Where was all this coming from?

As a result of the meeting, they placed me on a performance improvement plan for one year, which was a double whammy for me. They could not place me on probation because I was already vested with the government. Nevertheless, it felt like probation to me.

After my anger subsided and I did a little self-reflection, I must admit some of what was said was not far from the truth. I realized that I had unresolved anger issues, which led me to react before thinking. However, as far as I was concerned, I was not aggressive. I simply spoke the truth when necessary, even if it was not well-received.

At that time, I was a purchasing agent, which

meant I procured everything the scientists and administrative offices needed to run their labs and offices. This work mentally exhausted me, particularly at the end of the fiscal year, when the allocated budget must be spent. I was not always my friendly self during that time. Perhaps that's when it was most difficult to work with me. After ten years in the role, I was burned out and ready for a change. However, since I was serving a two-year probation sentence, I decided to stay there until the probation period was over.

As if probation from the court and my job weren't enough, I continued to play Russian roulette with my drug tests. You would think I learned my lesson from the positive drug test at my pretrial meetings. Well, I did not. I continued to snort cocaine throughout my probation period. Whenever I was contacted for a random test, my results were clean. All I can say is that God takes care of fools and babies, and I was not a baby.

CHAPTER
FIFTEEN

Y2K was most known as the year the internet was supposed to crash at the start of the new millennium. But we all know that didn't happen. Nevertheless, the year 2000 was memorable for several reasons.

First, I began an extensive search for a new job. If I were still a purchasing agent at the end of the year, it would not be because I didn't try to find a new position. Secondly, I became a grandmother in July when Akosua gave birth to Jabari Akeem, the first of my six grandchildren. Lastly, my probation came to an end in October. I felt good about what happened that year. Life was really good to me.

To add to the memories of that year, I had many changes occur in my life. The court-mandated therapy sessions helped me to realize that I spent a lot of time and energy focused on Mister and how to keep him. I also realized my kids were a big part of my identity as well. Between Mister and my kids, I put my dreams and desires on the back burner. I needed to find myself at this point.

I returned to college as the first step to focus on me and not my kids or Mister. College was a dream deferred for me. My job agreed to pay for courses related to my work. So, I searched for classes that fit my desired degree and met the criteria for my job. I took several courses that year and thrived in all of them. Then, I applied for every position I thought I was qualified for and proudly added the college classes to my resume.

Despite my efforts, I did not receive any interviews. I finally caught a break when I applied for a grants technical assistant position within my agency. I received a call to come in for the interview. When I arrived, I ran into a former lab worker for whom I once ordered supplies and materials. The interview went well, and I left feeling like the job was mine.

HR called and offered me the grants position at the beginning of December.

Before the woman could finish asking if I would accept the position, I excitedly shouted, "Yes!"

The position was a lateral move rather than a promotion, so I had to stay in my current position for thirty days instead of the normal two weeks allowed when leaving a job. But that didn't matter to me. What mattered the most was that my prayer was answered.

I had received the blessing of a new job before the year ended. Through the faithfulness of God, I started the position shortly after the new year in 2001. I had just enough sense to know all the positive changes in my life were not of my doing, but I still didn't turn my face completely toward God.

The more things changed, the more they stayed the same. With my probation over and my record expunged, it was time to P-A-R-T-Y! Mister and I fell back into our normal routine. My cocaine and weed connections stayed on speed dial, and I added my love for German beer to the mix.

My financial situation became such a mess that I filed for Chapter Eleven bankruptcy by mid-2001. At the suggestion of my bankruptcy attorney, I found a part-time job to help pay my bankruptcy trustee. For three years, I thought I was a superwoman because I worked a full-time and part-time job, raised my kids, and attended college part-time. I never felt such a sense of purpose like I did over those three years. I managed to do all of this while I continued to date and party with Mister. This sense of accomplishment gave me more confidence and self-assurance.

Life was good once again, so good that I partied during the week and the weekends. However, the frequent partying took a toll on me. I spent many nights snorting coke, smoking weed, and drinking beer.

It's so crazy when I think about what I did. I would binge solo and with friends; it didn't matter. The stimuli from coke made me soar like an eagle and feel invincible. Then the weed, a depressant, mellowed me out, and the beer quenched my thirst and boosted my high. Man, what was I thinking?

I was too tired to do anything except sleep after I binged all night. My work attendance began to suffer. I called out often because I had only slept a few hours. I could count on one hand, with fingers left over, the number of people who knew I was addicted to cocaine. My friends knew I smoked weed, but snorting coke was something totally different. I kept that knowledge from my friends, but it didn't stop them from being impacted by my habit.

Once, I told a friend I would take her to a shopping center in Baltimore. I was tired that morning because I pulled a solo all-nighter. I normally slept late on Saturday mornings when I binged the night before, but I made a promise to my friend. So, as tired and hungover as I was, I drove us to Baltimore.

At some point, I left my friend in the store and went back to sleep in my car. I slept for several hours, and my friend didn't know where I was or where the car was parked. When I finally woke up, I found her sitting on a bench, pissed off at me. I apologized for not telling her I was going to the car to sleep. Needless to say, my friend never asked me to shop with her again.

By 2005, not much had changed in my life. I continued to snort coke, smoke weed, drink alcohol, and sleep with Mister. But something was shifting within me. I grew sick and tired of being sick and tired. I was literally sick from snorting so much cocaine.

I became concerned about what was being used to cut the coke. I heard that dealers were using talcum powder, rat poison, or anything they could get their hands on to decrease purity and to create more product to sell. Not really knowing what was being used to cut the coke, I began to think about the harmful effects it could have on my body. I read a magazine article about a woman who snorted for about ten years. There were undeniable similarities we shared. Both of us were single and involved with married men. That article tremendously affected me.

The woman in the article stopped doing coke by the power of prayer. I thought if she could do it, so could I. So, on a cold, dreary day in November, I got on my knees and told God I was tired of making myself sick and that I did not want to snort cocaine anymore, but I did not have the strength to stop on my own. This problem was bigger than me, and I needed His help. God heard me and answered my prayer. I have not used cocaine since that November day in 2005. However, my use of other "street pharmaceuticals" would not end for a few more years.

I tried to fill the void in my life with drugs, sex, and alcohol, but they were all the wrong things. I began to seriously think about my life and purpose. In the stillness of the early morning hours and the quietness of the house, I began to read the bible and pray. Honestly, I didn't understand everything I read, but I continued to read and pray as part of my early morning routine. Over time, this routine began to comfort me.

No, my life didn't magically get better, but despite the chaos in my life, something happened inwardly. What I didn't understand at that time was my faith was growing, even though I lived in constant sin. My response to life's circumstances and situations was different now. When things became too hard, unbearable, or painful, both physically and emotionally, my first instinct was to pray about the situation.

For example, one morning, I woke up in pain from a boil on my butt. The boil was painful when I sat and walked. That morning, I got on my knees and asked God to take away the pain. Then, I got dressed and drove to work. Once at work, I began to drink water. The more water I drank, the more I went to the bathroom. By the time I got home that evening, I was not in pain, and the boil had shrunk in size.

God had answered my prayer and removed the pain. I could not say anything but thank you, Lord. I realized a few things that day. One that my faith had grown. Two, that the power of prayer is real, and three, that daily water intake is essential.

That day with the boil was preparation for the next big faith moment to come. When I woke up in pain one November morning in 2011, it was a no-brainer as to what I needed to do next. My stomach hurt something fierce, and I hadn't felt pain like that since 2007, when I discovered I had gallstones and needed to have my gallbladder removed.

In the words of the Christian singer Tye Tribbett, "If He did before, He can do it again!"

Well, I went to God in prayer on my knees, but this time it was different. A feeling came over me.

Without thinking, I uttered, "I receive you, Father."

I heard the Holy Spirit say, "Leave Mister alone."

Immediately, I said, "No, I can't do that."

Foolish Me! Who did I think I was to tell God no? I didn't know what to think about my experience that morning. For a few days, I asked myself if I had been saved that day. Eventually, I realized that I had received salvation that day. So, at fifty-four years old, God extended His grace and mercy to my wretched soul.

I traveled to North Carolina with some friends to see the Baltimore Ravens play against the Carolina Panthers shortly after I got saved. We drove down on a Saturday afternoon, checked into our hotel, and met with local friends for dinner and drinks. I turned in early because I was tired.

I woke up early Sunday morning and turned on the television. There was a preacher I had never seen before on the broadcast, and as a new babe in Christ, what he said made so much sense to me. I later learned the preacher was Pastor Charles Stanley, a nationally renowned pastor with a worldwide ministry. Since I didn't have a church home, I began to watch him on Sunday mornings once I returned home.

CHAPTER
SIXTEEN

My daughter Akosua and her four children moved back home with me in December 2011. The children's ages ranged from 2 to 11 years, and she was also separated from her husband.

Mental health is nothing to play with and can be a beast if left untreated. That is what happened with Akosua. Little did I know, depression caused her to experience apathy, laziness, and lack of motivation. I came home each day after work to dirty dishes and dinner unprepared, which was more than I could handle. Daily arguments ensued.

I screamed at her, "Get off your lazy behind and find a job."

That was until the day she broke down in tears and told me she needed help. She took a magazine quiz and determined that she might be depressed. At that moment, I no longer complained but listened. Together, we made a plan to get her therapy, which she did. Eventually, Akosua realized she was depressed and suffered from postpartum depression. Double whammy!

The cloud of depression began to lift after several months with the aid of her therapist. As time passed and Akosua continued therapy, she felt better and found a job. But it did not happen overnight. It took a couple of years for her to get back on her feet, but she continuously showed up for herself and made the necessary changes. For that, I was so very proud of her.

This all in itself was a lesson for me. Things are almost never as they appear. Sometimes, you have to take time to step back, listen, and see the whole picture. Oftentimes, we miss key information because we look through magnifying glasses instead of single lenses. No one knew what she was going through, but God did. She went through something long before she moved back home, and no one saw the signs. Thank God He worked it out for her to move back home.

In 2012, I struggled with my newfound salvation. I attempted to navigate my own life while I tried to help my daughter. However, the truth was that I was doing life on my own terms. I was still drinking, drugging, and sexing Mister. Oh man, was I conflicted.

I knew I wanted to fully embrace my salvation, but as a babe in Christ, I didn't have the right support system around me. The pull of life as I knew it was way too strong of a current for me. So, I gave in and lived life on my terms. I DID NOT WANT TO LET GO!

My mother informed me in April 2013 that my sister hosted bible study meetings in the basement of their home on Wednesday evenings. Little did she know, they were an answer to my prayers and desire to learn more about Jesus. On June 16, 2013, that small gathering became the Remnant of God Deliverance Ministry, Inc.

We held our first worship service on Father's Day, and what an appropriate day to praise and worship our Heavenly Father. Those bible study meetings were a godsend. I initially attended the meetings to support my sister, but I quickly realized it was really for me. She was the vessel God used to get me in church. I noticed a major difference in my life within my first year of regular church attendance.

It was about this time that a gnawing and nagging feeling grew within me. It was the conviction of my disobedience. God told me to leave Mister alone, but I refused. The more I learned about Jesus and God, the more the feeling grew. But the stubbornness within me made me feel like I knew better than God. Mister was to be mine.

Oh, leave it to God to show you better than He can tell you. In December of 2014, Mister got married, and our relationship came full circle. When I met Mister, he was married, then he got divorced. Now, all these years later, he was married again, and it wasn't to me.

Once again, I was not chosen. However, it wasn't a surprise.

While I may have been exclusive to Mister, he was not to me. I knew this, but the tie that bonded us had me in such a way that I would take him any way I could get him. At some point earlier that year, Mister told me he had decided to marry Ms. Goodie, the other woman he had been seeing.

I told him, "Well, just don't tell me until after you've married her because I don't think I can handle knowing the date beforehand."

He replied, "I won't. I promise."

True to his word, he notified me by text after they were married.

In January of 2015, Mister and I agreed to finally call it quits. I mean, it had to be over. He was a newlywed, and my pride would not allow me to be second yet again. Well, at least not for a few months. As always, our break was short-lived. By April, we were back in each other's arms and picked up where we left off. All the while, I tried to ignore the conviction that grew in my soul. I was addicted to him, and the two of us back together felt like it was meant to be.

Aunt Frances was taken to the hospital in late September of 2015. It had been a few years since I last saw her. There was a time when I would randomly drop in to see her, but when her health began to decline, she no longer welcomed visitors. On October 1st, I was sitting at work when I had an overwhelming feeling to visit Aunt Frances in the hospital. I still worked in Montgomery County, but she was in the hospital in southern Prince George's County. So, I left work at 1:00 pm for the hour-long drive to the hospital.

When I entered the hospital room, I didn't recognize my aunt. You see, I expected to see the vibrant woman I had known all my life. However, there laid a woman who was a shell of what I remembered. I cried and told her how much I missed and loved her, but Aunt Frances suffered from dementia and didn't recognize me.

That is until I said, "Aunt Frances, I'm Carla."

Instantly, her eyes lit up, and she responded, "You belong to me!"

She knew then that we had a familial connection. I sat with Aunt Frances for a few hours while she slept. It didn't matter to me that we did not talk. What mattered most was that I was with my dearly loved aunt.

Early on the morning of October 18th, I called Regina to confirm our plans that my grandson Jabari and I would pick her up after church to visit Aunt Frances. My sister Karen called me as I prepared for church, letting me know that Aunt Frances had passed. Our plans immediately shifted. We decided I would come to church so my mother, Karen, and Connie, a church family member, and I could go together to inform Regina.

Karen made a courtesy call and informed Regina's pastor about Aunt Frances' passing. She asked that they not tell her until we arrived. In record time, we drove from Baltimore County, MD, to Prince George's County, which was an hour away. Upon our arrival at the church, we were greeted by the pastor and the church administrator, who escorted me and Karen to our Aunt Regina.

Regina thought we were there to pick her up for the hospital visit. When she got in the car, my mother told her Aunt Frances had died. We went to the hospital, which was not far away, to say our final goodbyes. When I look back on that time, I realize the Holy Spirit nudged me to visit Aunt Frances a few days earlier because He knew it would be my last time to see her alive. Thank You, Holy Spirit, for giving me that time with her.

A few months after Aunt Frances' passing, I woke up and realized I couldn't continue with Mister anymore. I thought I was in bliss, but the conviction of my disobedience had become more than I could bear. I mean, really, who did I think I was to defy God like that? Not only did I verbalize my no, but my actions, thoughts, and deeds told God no. I mean, I was fully committed to this act of disobedience.

In essence, I was a hypocrite. I professed to love the Lord; all the while, I did the devil's bidding. I must have fallen and bumped my head. As the old folks would say, "I knew my arms were too short to box with God," yet I continually tried to throw jabs at His will. My life was the perfect example of the Mark 26:41 scripture; my spirit was willing, but my flesh was unwilling to yield.

I confessed my weakness to God on several occasions because I knew I wasn't strong enough to leave the relationship on my own. The Bible says He gives strength to the weary and power to the weak (Isaiah 40:29). Well, I really needed God to be my strength. Once I began to yield my will, God began to show me that He had a time and place for everything. That day, I began the process of surrendering my will to God. It didn't happen overnight, but I started the process.

CHAPTER
SEVENTEEN

Our church fall revival was held in November 2018. It was spirit-filled and spirit-led.

The prophetic word I received during the service said, "The Lord is working on the heart of an older gentleman in your life."

Immediately, I thought of Mister. I just knew that meant Mister would see the error of his ways, and we would finally be together. But God had other plans.

A few months later, in January, our church held a corporate Daniel Fast. I decided to participate and fasted from 6:00 am to 6:00 pm for twenty-one days. I did not eat or drink anything other than water during those hours. After the core fast hours, I only ate fruits, vegetables, and nuts. I received clarity like never before while on the fast.

In a conversation with Mister, I said, "I love you,

but not more than I love the Lord. And my relationship with you is important to me, but not more important than my relationship with God."

Shocked, he said, "Wow, I've never heard you talk like this before."

I knew the Lord's strength enabled me to say those things to Mister. Before the fast, I already had those thoughts but was too afraid to tell him out of fear of losing him.

The fast was just the beginning. In March, I received a call from Mister.

He said, "My wife confronted me and said she knows I'm cheating on her. I don't know what to do. I don't want to hurt her, and I don't want to lose you."

I did not want the relationship to end either, but I knew it was the right thing to do, not to mention it was past time. In the end, he chose not to hurt his wife. I would be lying if I said I wasn't hurt because I was. A part of me wanted him to choose me, but I understood that Mister was her husband, and if he left her for me, he would leave me for someone else.

Mister and I said "I love you" to each other. I told him I would miss him and then said goodbye for the last time. My heart ached as I cried and mourned the loss of my lover and friend. By no means was it easy to say goodbye. We were friends and lovers for thirty-three years. Some people don't even stay married that long.

The first few months of the breakup, I was like a

junkie detoxing. I waited for the phone to ring to hear his voice on the other end. I just knew I would get my happy Mother's Day call or text, but nope, it did not happen. When August came, I anxiously awaited his call with well wishes and plans for my birthday. To my disappointment, he never called. By Christmas, it was clear that it was truly over this time. Although I longed for him and missed him terribly, God was faithful and kept me.

Wednesday, September 25, 2019, began like any other day. I woke up, read the Bible and my devotionals, and prayed, as was my new daily routine. I arrived at work around 6:30 am and started my workday as usual. My work phone rang around 9:30 am. It was Jackie, Aunt Regina's goddaughter.

She said, "Nailah, the rehabilitation center just called and said Regina is unresponsive."

Immediately, I screamed and began to cry. The rest of what happened seemed surreal. Ms. P, my branch chief; Ms. F, my supervisor; and several co-workers came to my cubicle and consoled me. All I could do was point to the phone and continue to cry. Ms. P got on the phone with Jackie and was told about my aunt. My first instinct was to call and tell my mother and my sister. Ms. P was kind enough to allow me to make my emergency phone calls in the privacy of her office.

When I spoke with my sister Karen, she offered to tell our mother. She suggested we meet at the rehab center.

Before Karen hung up, she said, "Nailah, pray. Just pray."

I hung up with Karen, and Ms. P and Ms. F offered to pray with me. Ms. P led the prayer, and while she prayed, God spoke to me, and His words brought me peace and comfort.

God said, "She's with me. She loves you, and she knows you love her."

Quietly, I thanked Him for the message, blew Aunt Regina a kiss, and said goodbye to her.

When the prayer was over, I told the ladies, "She is no longer here, and I'm ok with that."

The ladies offered to go with me to the rehab center, as I was unsure I could make the hour-long drive to the rehab center without breaking down in tears. Ms. P drove my car while Ms. F followed behind us in her car. This way, Ms. P would have a way back to work. Karen called while we were in the car and said Aunt Regina had passed. Thankfully, God had already told me and given me peace.

Regina's birthday was a few months prior, on July 13th, and we made lunch plans to celebrate. The hospital scheduled her for surgery four days later, so I invited family and friends to join us for a surprise birthday lunch. I arrived at Regina's apartment about one in the afternoon and drove her to the bank. We also went to Target to keep her occupied until our scheduled reservation time. I had a good time laughing and joking with her that day.

When we finally arrived at the restaurant, she was so surprised to see the family and friends who gathered to celebrate her.

She looked at me and said, "You got me."

Jackie and I went with Aunt Regina on the day of her surgery. The surgery was successful. However, two weeks later, during her follow-up appointment, she passed out in the doctor's office, and they rushed her to the emergency room. The hospital admitted Regina to the hospital, and it was during this stay that she developed an infection, which caused her stay to be extended by a few weeks.

The hospital transferred Aunt Regina to a rehabilitation center in Landover, MD, upon her release from the hospital. I visited Regina often while she was in the rehab center. I took my granddaughter Jaz with me the last time I visited with her. When I entered the room, Regina looked tired.

We had a pleasant visit. Regina was an avid sports fan and was watching a college football game on TV. I took pictures of her and Jaz together, and we talked about her upcoming doctor's appointment. I assured her I would meet her at the doctor's office and that Jackie would ride with her from the rehab center to the appointment. I ensured she had enough to eat and helped her pick her outfit for the appointment before we left.

As I said goodbye to Aunt Regina, I hugged and kissed her.

I said, "I love you."

Aunt Regina replied with her signature phrase, "Love you more."

Who knew that Saturday would be my last time seeing my aunt alive? God knew, and I am so glad I was blessed to spend that day with my aunt. I have peace and comfort knowing that she knew how much I loved her and that she is with the Lord.

CHAPTER
EIGHTEEN

January 1, 2020, began a year of challenges. Within three months of the New Year, the world plunged into a global pandemic, COVID-19. It was as if God took the world by the shoulder and shook it fervently to get our attention. I prayed daily for the well-being of all those I knew and loved because the virus was highly contagious. I prayed for my community and the world at large. I especially prayed for those who lost their lives and those afflicted by the virus. I cannot speak for anyone else, but HE, God, certainly got my attention.

A few months before the pandemic, Artise, who had moved to Alabama, and I spoke regularly by phone. He shared with me that he had some health issues.

I asked Artise, "Would you consider coming back

to the DC area so your family can help provide you with support and care?"

I knew his children and family members in the Washington, DC area would help adequately care for him.

He said, "Well, I guess it's something to consider."

Ultimately, I believe the thought of being away from his family throughout the pandemic finally convinced him to return to the area.

Akosua and I pitched in to purchase a plane ticket for Artise to return to DC. The plan was for his niece to pick him up and drive him to their aunt's house.

About a week before his arrival, as I prayed in the shower, I heard God say to let Artise stay with me.

I cried, "No, Lord! That is not what I want to do!"

Immediately, I had a check in my spirit as I remembered the last time I actively disobeyed God, and I did not want to be disobedient again.

I quickly gathered myself and said, "Not my will, but Your will, Lord."

I was in the shower again a few days later and prayed to God.

I asked, "God, why do you want me to invite Artise to live in my home?"

I felt like I wasn't prepared and could not do what He asked of me. Then, God brought back something I heard my pastor say to my remembrance.

She said, "When God gives you an assignment, He

equips you with what you need to complete the assignment."

Everyone, including Artise, was surprised when I told him he could stay with me and that our grandsons, Jabari and Javonte, and I would pick him up when he arrived. After we changed his travel schedule and mode of transportation, Artise arrived late on the night of May 8th at Union Station in Washington, DC.

Artise and I now lived under the same roof for the first time in thirty-five years. Our grandchildren enjoyed having their "Pop-pop" with us. I liked that Artise was a great cook and he enjoyed cooking for the family. However, I did have to lay down a few rules.

I did not allow cigarette smoking or excessive alcohol consumption in my home. Don't get me wrong, I occasionally enjoy a glass of wine or wine spritzer, but I have a low to no tolerance for drunkenness, and Artise both smoked and drank. To help him feel at home, I took him to the liquor store for beer and cigarettes. I conceded to let him smoke and drink only in the backyard after I saw him do the same on my front steps a few times.

One day, while I waited for Artise to walk out of the liquor store, I realized I was aiding and abetting his unhealthy habits. As a diabetic and someone with a family history of lung disorders, the last thing he needed to do was smoke and drink.

So, I said to him, "While I don't mind taking you where you want to go, I can no longer take you to the liquor store or to buy cigarettes. I cannot continue to help you do further harm and damage to your health."

In the first weeks of him living with us, Artise and I had conversations about our lives. I would tell him about my life since being saved and how reading the bible, attending church regularly, and praying helped me greatly. I shared how my life was imperfect, but my faith and trust in God carried me through my trials and tribulations.

We continued conversing about spiritual growth, and I shared my books about spiritual development with him. Like most churches in the country, my church held worship services via Facebook, as we could not worship in person during the early part of the pandemic. This was great because it allowed Artise to watch services with me from time to time.

We kicked the summer off with a backyard cookout to celebrate Javonte's birthday and Memorial Day. The guest list was small because the state of Maryland didn't permit large gatherings for safety due to the pandemic during this time. But we managed to still have a good time.

We celebrated Father's Day the following month and prepared everything Artise wanted for dinner. We gave him a present that I know he cherished because it came from his daughter and grandchildren with love. It was the first time in 38 years that Artise celebrated Father's Day with his daughter. I knew this moment was special for both him and Ko.

Shortly after July 4th, Artise spent time with his aunt and cousins. He was usually drunk when he returned home. Note that my tolerance for drunkenness at this point in my life was extremely low to the point of non-existent. Since he did not drink in the house, there was nothing I could really say. After all, he was a grown man, and who was I to police him?

By October, we had reached the straw that would break the camel's back. One evening, Jabari and his girlfriend, Ryjae, brought Artise home from his aunt's just as me, Ko, and the kids were leaving to go to the mall. As usual, he was drunk. When we returned a few hours later, I found my front door unlocked and slightly ajar. The first thing that came to mind was that Artise, in a drunken state, had left home and left the door open.

We walked inside and saw Jabari and Ryjae struggling as they lifted Artise off the floor from an apparent fall. Artise was a big man in stature and weight, so this was not easy.

Jabari said to us, "After we left, he called and said he fell down the steps and asked us to come back to help him get up."

Relieved it was not a security breach, I looked around to ensure everything was still intact. I noticed a vase that I owned for years had been broken during Artise's fall. While I was partly upset by my irreplaceable broken vase, most of my anger stemmed from Artise's drunken state. Jabari apologized for the vase and promised to replace it. Still, it was not his fault or responsibility to do so.

Out of nowhere, Artise said, "Jabari, take me back to my aunt's. I can't stay here anymore."

Confused, I said, "Take you back to your aunt's house? You just came back from over there, and she lives an hour away. Don't you think that's a little insensitive?"

An argument ensued as I continued to break down the many ways I felt Artise was inconsiderate of everyone's time and energy who had tried to help him. Eventually, he left, and Jabari and Ryjae drove him back to his aunt's.

When they left, I felt like I had failed God. The assignment He gave me was to lead Artise back to Him. Guilt consumed me because I felt like a failure. I spoke with a dear friend who helped me realize I had not failed, as there was never a time limit to complete the assignment. Perhaps I mistakenly believed the deadline needed to be before Artise moved out of my home.

It was a great thing when Artise moved in with his aunt. We made amends, and our friendship continued to grow. He eventually transitioned to his own apartment, and life moved forward. How wrong I was to put a limit on God? God's work is a continual process and always in progress.

CHAPTER NINETEEN

There were many changes and challenges throughout the first year of the COVID-19 pandemic. There were no in-person family gatherings for the holidays, and almost all gatherings took place virtually via Zoom, Google Meet, or Microsoft TEAMS. It was certainly an adjustment and a difficult time.

A few of my friends and close relatives encountered this insidious virus. My family skipped the Thanksgiving Zoom in 2020 because my sister Karen was sick with COVID. My church family and our biological family prayed for her healing. We also prayed for my mother's protection from the virus since they lived in the same house.

I took comfort because, although Karen was sick, she did not need hospitalization. That meant she had a good fighting chance to win the battle over the virus.

Well, the fervent prayers of the righteous prevailed. Karen fully recovered, and my mother did not contract COVID.

God never ceases to amaze me. While I prayed for my sister and mother, God spoke to me about my next assignment.

As I sat still in prayer and meditation, I heard the Holy Spirit say, "There is a book in you. Write about your journey to salvation."

Never in my wildest dreams had I thought about writing a book. I didn't know when or how, but I trusted God and knew He would let me know when to move forward—all praises to Yahweh-Rapha, the Lord who heals.

Christmas brought a semblance of normalcy to our family. We scheduled our Christmas family dinner online via Zoom to comply with local government regulations. We met prior to Christmas day and exchanged gifts to open during the dinner call. On Christmas Day at 3:00 p.m., we prayed, ate, played games, and opened our gifts.

They canceled our annual Watch Night Service on New Year's Eve (NYE) as the pandemic restricted in-person services. I must admit, I was a little bummed about that. I spent the past few years on NYE in church, as it allowed me to praise God collectively with others. We gave praise to God for his protection through the year's trials and tribulations and His blessings for the new year.

Don't get me wrong, I praise God every day. However, considering how I used to spend NYE in the past, bringing in the New Year with prayer and worship was now a staple in my life. The canceled church services forced me to watch endless NYE television shows. To tell the truth, I almost missed the New Year coming in because I fell asleep. I woke up at 11:55 p.m. just in time to see the ball drop in Times Square.

I received a financial windfall in January 2021, which allowed me to pay half of my yearly church-building pledge and increase my tithe contribution. I worked on the church's administrative staff and assisted in other areas as needed. It felt good to meet my personal financial needs and also sow into the kingdom of God.

I remember having a conversation with my sister about the spiritual growth I felt taking place in my life.

I said, "I can feel myself changing on the inside, even though it hasn't manifested externally."

Karen said, "That's ok. Internally is where the Holy Spirit does the work of transforming us into the image of Christ."

That was confirmation I was where I was supposed to be.

Not too long after, Karen called. I didn't think much of it because she is my sister and we talk regularly. But on this day, she didn't just call as my sister. She called me as my pastor.

She said, "I've been watching you, and I've seen your spiritual growth and faithfulness to God and our church over the years. I would like for you to join the board of trustees. You don't have to give me an answer right away. Take your time to think and pray about your decision."

My first thought was of how much of an honor it was to be considered for the position. Then, I took the time to consult God for His thoughts about the position. About a week later, I called Karen and accepted the trustee position.

The next morning, during my quiet time with God, the Holy Spirit said, "Be on guard. You're under spiritual attack."

Later that day, my cousin Gerald and I got in my car. I mistakenly left the window on the passenger side down when it rained the night before. The rain soaked the carpet floor mat.

Immediately, I heard, "This is an attack."

I would not have thought of this as an attack if God had not already warned me. This incident happened on a Wednesday, and it caused me to think about other incidents that happened shortly before I accepted the trustee position.

On Monday of that week, I went to Costco with Gerald to purchase a new phone. My old phone somehow erased all my data. I was distraught because

I lost my personal notes, including the journal I kept of every time I had an experience with God. I was devastated that those notes were forever lost. Although this happened before I officially accepted the position, God showed me how the spiritual attack began even before I accepted the trustee role.

As I sat in the car with Gerald and realized how this all tied together, I decreed, "The devil is a liar!"

Gerald looked at me, confused, until I explained how everything came together. He fully understood. Fortunately, I have an excellent memory of things that are important to me. I remembered some, if not most, of what was lost in the data erasure. As hard as Satan tried, he could not thwart what God planned for the faithful believer, and I AM A FAITHFUL BELIEVER.

I woke up the morning of May 10, 2021, with the desire to be obedient heavy on my heart. The assignment to write about my salvation journey was strong, but I did not know where to begin. I knew God would not give me an assignment he didn't equip me to complete.

So, I began to recite my favorite scripture, Proverbs 3:5-6, "Trust in the Lord with all thine heart. Lean not to thy own understanding. Acknowledge Him in thine ways, and He shall direct thy path."

The following week, I still felt angst and discontentment in my spirit because of my disobedience to God. I was plagued with insecurities and doubts. While in the shower, I heard the lyrics to one of my favorite songs that talked about being victorious with God. I knew I needed to push past my doubts and insecurities. God gave me the assignment almost a year prior, and I still had not put pen to paper. I allowed fear and procrastination to rob me of time.

One Sunday morning, I arrived at church not quite feeling like my normal jovial self. I did not realize my downward countenance showed while I was in Sunday School. I realized God used the testimonies of the class members to minister to me (God is so awesome and always shows up when we need Him). I shared with them I felt insecure and how it kept me from completing God's assignment.

I did not tell them what the assignment was.

Kandyce, my niece and Sunday school instructor, said, "I knew something was wrong because you did not seem like yourself. I prayed for God to deliver you from anxiety attacks."

I cried as I listened to her testimony. Immediately, Kandyce stopped the lesson and asked everyone to pray for me. The entire class laid their hands on me and prayed with me and for me. The outpouring of love was so special. I felt deliverance from the insecurities and doubts in that moment.

I was so excited after church that I called my friend Sherri because I knew she was writing a book and could offer advice. She told me that our mutual friend, T Lynn, could help me write and publish my book. I contacted T Lynn, and in our first meeting, I confided my feelings of terror about this assignment and my fears of vulnerability.

She asked me to share my qualities, and I rattled off a few. She told me my militant spirit was that of a fighter/warrior, and I would use that same spirit to fight on behalf of God's people. She suggested I read Possessing the Gates of the Enemy, which details how to battle spiritual warfare.

Later, while in the shower, I asked God if being an intercession warrior was His will for my life and my kingdom assignment. He responded yes, and as soon as I accepted the assignment, I stumbled but did not fall. As I regained my footing, I realized God's revelation was I may stumble, but I will not fall. Satan would try to attack me physically and spiritually.

As I began writing the book in July 2021, I wondered, "Who was I to think anyone would be interested in reading my story?" I started walking in my neighborhood as a way to clear my mind. Walking and communing with God allowed me to let go of the anxiety I had, if only for a few moments. During one of those walks, God told me this book would bring salvation to many people. I had a renewed desire to write the book. After all, God had my back.

As long as I am disobedient, God cannot use me to His fullest extent, purpose, and glory. I was not willing to live in disobedience by not writing this book. Although I had self-doubt, I wrote all summer. Whenever the doubt overwhelmed me, I leaned on God. He reassured me that He was always with me.

I took a girls' weekend trip to Myrtle Beach that August for my birthday. One night, I dreamt of the names of two little girls, Jessica and Elizabeth Maldonado. I knew they were sisters, perhaps twins. Upon awakening, I asked God if He wanted me to pray for the Maldonado girls, as I did not know them. He said pray for them, which I did before I went back to sleep. In the book Possessing the Gates of the Enemy, it reads, "Prayer warriors should pray for people they do not know, the local community and the world."

This was the first of many people I prayed for that came to me in dreams. In the beginning, I did not know what to do. Now I know that if I have a dream about someone I know or the names of people I do not know come to me, I pray for them. I do not know their needs, circumstances, or what they are going through, but I trust God does. I obediently pray for their protection, strength, and perseverance to endure whatever the situation.

I stated previously that God never ceases to amaze me. In late October, my vehicle's check engine light came on. My first thought was I had to get the oil changed. So I took it to a local auto shop only to be told the head gasket was about to blow. They advised me that the age of my vehicle (2011) and the high mileage (over 200K miles) were not worth spending thousands of dollars on a new engine. I mentioned to a few people that my retirement vehicle would be an Acura RDX. However, I hadn't planned to purchase it until fall 2022.

It was a coincidence that I started researching earlier in the year for my planned purchase. I wanted a sense of how much it would cost so that I could save the money needed for my purchase. Now, here is where my awesome God manifested Himself.

This vehicle purchase was not something that I asked or prayed for. But God cares for all our needs and wants. They approved my auto loan with a low interest rate one day after I completed the online application. The low interest rate was crucial because rate increases occurred over the next few months. They delivered my RDX to my home on November 8th, a year ahead of my timeline.

Refinancing my mortgage and combining the home equity line of credit (HELOC) for a lower interest rate also crossed my mind. My mortgage rate was about 5.25%, and the HELOC's variable rate ballooned to almost 6%. The monthly payment became challenging to meet. I prayed for guidance in this process. I immediately received an email from my current mortgage holder to refinance my mortgage.

All I could do was say, "Thank you, Lord."

He answered that prayer request instantly.

I started the loan process in mid-November and received my mortgage approval in January. Upon its completion, God reduced my interest rate to less than

5%, and the monthly payment increased by only three dollars. That was inclusive of the HELOC. I know this was the favor and blessing of God.

Satan is furious when believers receive favor and blessings from God. He throws fiery darts toward the believer to try to thwart all God has bestowed. In my case, Satan attacked me physically. I worked from home like most people due to the pandemic, and on the afternoon of December 14th, I took my lunch break around 1:30 p.m.

My right ankle rolled under me as I stepped down the stairs, which caused me to fall. My ankle began to swell immediately as the pain shot up my leg from the ankle to the knee. I could not stand, let alone walk. Fortunately, my granddaughter, Jania, was home from school and called her mother to take me to urgent care.

I hobbled to the car with borrowed crutches and rode to the nearest urgent care center. X-rays revealed that I had fractured my fibula, so they referred me to an orthopedist specialist. A couple of days later, the specialist requested I remain bedridden for two weeks and keep my ankle elevated to reduce swelling. I was given a boot to wear for seven weeks on my second appointment with the orthopedic specialist.

Needless to say, I only left home when it was absolutely necessary. I missed church services and our first in-person Watch Night New Year's Eve service in two years. To my delight, the service was live on Facebook, so I attended virtually. It was not the same as being in church, but it was better than nothing at all. Even with this physical attack, Satan could not steal my joy.

My journey to salvation is not a destination. It is ongoing. I can see God's hand all over my life, particularly when it comes to my relationship with my mother. For as long as I can remember, I have loved my mother, but I did not always like her. I never quite felt like she loved me because she was not demonstrative or communicative with her affections. She showed her children with love through the provision of food, clothes, and shelter. She worked hard and tirelessly to ensure all of our needs and most of our wants were met. This, she instilled in my sister and I by her example.

The difference we both learned is the importance of telling your children you love them as well as provide for their basic needs. In my case, not hearing those three little words, "I love you," devastated me.

My mother and I bumped heads numerous times, often resulting in shouting matches. I felt guilty because I did not like her and often told her with my words or actions. I recall an argument we had when I was a teenager. I was living in her home at the time and doing my laundry. I do not remember what we argued about, but I recall my anger caused me to throw bleach on the clothes she had on.

I realized years later that I could have severely injured her. But at that moment, I did not care. My anger clouded all rational thoughts. In the years before I received salvation, I thought constantly about the fragile relationship with my mother and often referred to it as a "love-hate-love relationship" in my self-talk. I blamed myself for my angry outbursts and felt guilty for how I felt. Not liking my mother was also not honoring her.

I asked myself why I was so angry towards my mother and where the anger came from. I did not understand underneath my anger was all the hurt and pain left from my childhood trauma. I asked God to remove all animosity I had in my heart towards her as I recognized she did her very best raising her children.

As much as I prayed, I could not understand why I still felt anger and resentment toward my mother. One day, I received comfort from God when He assured me that some wounds are deep and take longer to heal.

My sister usually drives our mother home after our church services. This particular Sunday, Karen had an engagement and could not take her home. As I drove my mother home, an argument ensued. The dispute stemmed from my mother's trivial comment that I was negative because I disagreed with her. My mother accused me of negativity in the past for one reason or another, but that day, it rubbed me the wrong way.

After dropping her off, I wondered why I was so angry towards my mother. At that moment, I realized I had never really told her how I actually felt about her. I usually lashed out at her in anger. That was my Aha moment.

I decided to write her a letter. To my surprise, my mother called a few days later and stated she wanted to work towards a repaired relationship. I told her I desired that as well and shared that I was writing a letter to her. One may think the two of us wanting reconciliation was coincidental, but I know it was God's divine intervention.

I gave the letter to my mother at church the following Sunday. It took her a few days to respond to what I said in the letter. Initially, my mother tried to deny something that she did to me and tried to justify her behavior. This only infuriated me. I felt like she was negating my experiences and how I felt.

In the letter, I told her that I never heard words of encouragement. She consistently said mean, hurtful, and hateful things to me. I recounted the embarrassment and hurt I felt when she beat me in front of my best friend, Debbie, because she and I traded clothes. Lastly, I wrote that I never heard her say, "I love you," while growing up. It took my mother many years to verbally express, "I love you." I did not hear those words from her until I brought it to her attention. I was an adult with my own children when she finally told me she loved me.

Writing the letter was therapeutic. It revealed every crack in our relationship. It allowed me to release the pain, hurt, and anger. The letter let me have all my feelings, and most importantly, it helped me forgive my mother. The revelations in my letter led to several heated discussions. She eventually understood the pain I carried. She apologized for the hurt I experienced and shared that she did the best she knew how.

Our relationship is a continual work in progress. Yes, my mother still upsets me. However, when I feel my temper flare up, I quickly tell my mother I got to go. I also try to change the subject or simply do not respond. Not responding to her is better than an argument that ends in upset. I was sixty-five years "young" when I figured out my issues with my mother.

There is no doubt I love my mother. However, my mother wants a touchy/feely type of relationship from me, and I cannot give her something she did not or could not give me. We did not develop the relationship she wanted during my formative years. I love her the best way I know how and pray for the strength to love her wholeheartedly and affectionately. I do not expect this relationship to get better overnight. It will take both of us time, effort, and prayer to make it work.

From one of my earliest memories of setting myself on fire, God protected me. His consistent presence remained through all of my trials and tribulations. When I made foolish decisions and knowingly or unknowingly put myself in harm's way, God kept hurt, harm, and danger away from me. Since I received the gift of salvation, I have learned that FAITH is the key to living a victorious, abundant life.

Through the transformative and redemptive power of faith in Jesus Christ, life's hills and valleys are not as devastating as they were in the past. Faith stands beside you and replaces fear, insecurity, and failure with courage and boldness. I now possess a boldness that comes from knowing that through it all, God has my back, and there is no failure in leaning on and into GOD.

Without a relationship with God, I led a chaotic life filled with poor decisions and uncertainty. All I can say is Hallelujah! During those times when life becomes overwhelming, I am one of many who fall short of God's glory. God's grace allows me to repent, ask for and receive forgiveness, and start anew, seeking HIS glory.

Because of God's unconditional love for me and my faithfulness and love for HIM, there is power in knowing who God is and who I am in His eyes. I am A DAUGHTER OF THE MOST HIGH GOD, and HE has given me a crown of beauty for my ashes.

ABOUT THE AUTHOR

Nailah Agyemann was born and raised in the Washington, DC, Metropolitan area. She is a writer and a public servant with a thirty-six-year career in the government.

Nailah's love language is service, and she enjoys serving whenever and wherever she can. She finds the most joy in serving God and encouraging others while sharing her journey to becoming the woman that God created her to be.

Nailah is a founding member of the Remnant of

God Deliverance Ministry in Catonsville, Maryland, where she continues to serve in an administrative capacity. She lives in Montgomery County, Maryland, where she enjoys reading, traveling, and spending time with family & friends.

www.ingramcontent.com/pod-product-compliance
Lightning Source LLC
Chambersburg PA
CBHW051836090426
42736CB00011B/1830